Advocating Heightened Education

Critical Communication Pedagogy

Series Editors

Ahmet Atay, The College of Wooster

Deanna L. Fassett, San José State University

Critical pedagogy, as Cooks (2010), Freire (1970), and Lovaas, Baroudi and Collins (2002) argue, aims to empower and liberate individuals to achieve social change and transform oppressive and unequal social structures. This book series aims to contribute to the discourse of critical communication pedagogy by featuring works that utilize different dimensions of critical communication pedagogy to foster dialogue, to encourage self-reflexivity, and to promote social justice by allowing marginalized voices to be heard. Even though projects that focus on dynamics between teachers and students and their issues within classroom settings are crucial, this series aims to focus on works that utilize critical and cultural theories to interrogate the role of larger structures as they influence these relationships in higher education. Hence, in this series we will feature works that are built on critical communication pedagogy—works that function within a critical/cultural studies framework, and works that interrogate the notion of power, agency, dialogue and "voice" within the context of higher education and beyond. We argue that the work of educators and their educational philosophies are not limited to the classroom; hence, critical communication scholars are interested in connecting classroom pedagogy with its real life applications. Therefore, this series is interested in publishing work that captures these facets.

Titles in the series:

Advocating Heightened Education

Seeing and Inventing Academic Possibilities

Kathleen F. McConnell

LEXINGTON BOOKS
Lanham • Boulder • New York • London

Published by Lexington Books
An imprint of The Rowman & Littlefield Publishing Group, Inc.
4501 Forbes Boulevard, Suite 200, Lanham, Maryland 20706
www.rowman.com

6 Tinworth Street, London SE11 5AL, United Kingdom

British Library Cataloguing in Publication Information Available

Library of Congress Cataloging-in-Publication Data Available

ISBN 978-1-7936-0961-8 (cloth)
ISBN 978-1-7936-0962-5 (electronic)

Contents

Acknowledgments

I am grateful to the many people who supported this project, including Andrew Buckman, Paul Przybylowicz, John McLain, Terry Ford, Fran Horvath, and Angie Tran who helped me to arrange campus visits and locate documents. Thank you to everyone who generously lent me your time and stories including Bobbi Long, Dan Fernandez, Doug Schuler, Joli Sandoz, Laura Lee Lienk, Marla Elliott, Marsha Moroh, Arlene Haffa, Barbara Smith, Martha Henderson, Rita Pougiales, Rob Knapp, Sarah Pedersen, Sharon Anderson, Andrew Reece, Sherry Walton, Susan Preciso, Charles Pailthorpe, Michelle Aguilar Wells, Zoltan Grossman, John Berteaux, Gerald Shenk, Seth Pollack, Mingxia Li, and Thomas L. "Les" Purce.

This study would not have been possible without the assistance of Robin Guthrie, archivist at the Tanimura & Antle Family Memorial Library Archives and Special Collections at California State University Monterey Bay, Randy Stilson, archivist at the Malcolm Stilson Archives and Special Collections at The Evergreen State College, and Fordyce Williams, Coordinator of Archives and Special Collections at Clark University.

Portions of this project were presented to the Rhetoric Society of America, the Department of English at Indiana University, and the College of Social Sciences at San José State University. Thank you to Robert E. Terrill and Walter Jacobs for your invitations.

I am grateful for the support of SJSU's EdD Leadership Program and my encouraging peers at Lewis & Clark College's writing retreat hosted by Mitch Reyes.

Thank you also to my colleagues, former students, and friends who supported my work, most especially Brian Amsden, Ahmet Atay, Ruma Chopra, Deanna Fassett, Rebecca Friedberg, Mark Lieberman, Karen Lovass, Milene Monteiro, Keith Nainby, Nico Peck, and Sohinee Roy. Each of you contributed to this project. Thank you to Pat and Jim McConnell for your love, advice, insight, and enduring support. And finally, thank you to Amy Neymeyr, for everything.

Introduction

The semester before The Evergreen State College opened in 1971, Richard Nichols, Director of Information Services, welcomed new faculty with a history of Evergreen compiled from newspaper headlines. Summarizing articles from the *Daily Olympian* and other regional papers, Nichols gave a good-humored recap of the accolades the college had received and the controversies it had weathered in the four years since the state legislature had approved the campus. It was "a historical perspective," Nichols explained, "that you would have seen had you only looked at Evergreen by reading the newspapers."[1] In addition to the headlines, Nichols also shared details about the 990 acre campus, which was due to expand as the college bought "a little piece of property here and there to take care of drainage problems."[2] He closed with slides that showed the forested campus on the Olympic peninsula of Washington as it was in the spring of 1971, absent buildings or students and blanketed with Douglas Firs and trillium. "I just put [these photos] in here," he explained to the faculty, "to show you, to me, what really makes Evergreen as a campus Evergreen."[3]

Twenty-three years after Evergreen opened and eight hundred miles south along the Pacific coast line, the twelve founding faculty of the California State University, Monterey Bay (CSUMB) arrived in Seaside and moved into the houses previously occupied by the military families of Fort Ord, the decommissioned army base on which the university was to be built. Sharon S. Goldsmith, an ethnographer who observed the university's planning year, described the state of the 1,364 acre campus at the time: "situated on rolling dunes covered with scrub oaks are the university housing units. . . . Some [are] occupied by Department of Defense personnel; some are occupied by the growing university community; and many others are boarded up and home to scavenging wildlife—particularly skunks."[4] Marsha Moroh, former

1

Dean of the College of Science, Media Arts and Technology, remembers what inspired her to relocate in 1994 from the East Coast onto a base where "the army had literally walked out the door just weeks before."[5] "I loved the idea of trying to start a new university," she explained; "plus the opportunity; the army left the base and there was housing here and we thought about it as a living learning community."[6]

These details from the early days of Evergreen and CSUMB give a sense of the textured grounds on which education takes place. It is a level of detail so quirky, in fact, that it may seem too anecdotal to provide any insight into American higher education. Drainage issues and local wildlife are poor indicators of retention and graduation rates. A campus's acreage and faculty housing tell us little about post-graduate life. It is difficult to see in the anecdotal a grand mission underway to educate a nation and advance new knowledge. When viewed up close at the level of facilities management, higher education just looks convoluted, unwieldy, and expensive. Its messiness lends appeal to proposed reforms that are not bound by acreage, wrapped in amenities, or reliant on the changing tides of public funds.

Rising tuitions give good reason to wonder whether the cost of maintaining higher education's extensive infrastructure is worth it. In the wake of new media technologies, colleges and universities face unprecedented pressure to justify their infrastructure or eliminate it. A recent slate of reformers have proposed that we replace college campuses with decentralized offerings. Advocates of "unbundled education" cite the duplication, exclusivity, expense, and arbitrary bureaucracy of the traditional college experience. In *The End of College*, Kevin Carey argues that web-based technologies could potentially remake higher education into flexible degree programs divorced from institutions.[7] Carey offers a vision of a future in which students can attend what he calls the University of Everywhere to learn whatever they wish whenever they want so long as they demonstrate necessary competencies along the way. Anya Kamenetz and Richard A. DeMillo echo Carey and encourage us to pursue the possibilities that new media afford including the chance to eliminate both the generic bachelor's degree and the outdated techno-structural barriers that hinder the flow of information and knowledge.[8] Their proposals echo an old dream of education without schools. The most familiar iteration of that dream might be the 1997 film *Good Will Hunting*, which dramatized the desire to access knowledge directly without the drag of institutional filters. The film's autodidactic protagonist, Will Hunting, is gifted with a genius level IQ and a photographic memory. While working as a janitor at MIT, he comes to believe that college is more ornament than substance and that academia does not pursue knowledge so much as wraps it in prestige that we mistake for education.[9]

Anti-school sentiment, or the belief that education would improve if decoupled from its contrived settings, has proven an enduring trope. The persistent disillusionment with formal education assures anti-schoolers a reoccurring role in educational debates. Before Will Hunting, philosophers and polemicists, including Jean-Jacques Rousseau, Friedrich Nietzsche, Henry David Thoreau, Thorstein Veblen, and A. S. Neill, dreamed of education without the impositions of school.[10] In the 1970s, critics generated new reasons to imagine education beyond the campus. Colleges and universities, they argued, had become irrelevant either because they were too conservative or because they had caved to political trends. In *Academics in Retreat* (1971), Joseph Fashing and Steven E. Deutsch surveyed student unrest at six West Coast campuses and concluded that institutional innovation was "a defensive phenomenon" with reforms made "only grudgingly."[11] In *The Death of the American University* (1973), Louis G. Heller argued that academia had become "a monstrous fraud" by capitulating to "militants."[12] Both studies predicted that higher education's "haphazard" and "ill-planned" responses to change would prove fatal.[13] Carey taps the same sense of crisis and doom when he makes his case for the University of Everywhere.

The dream of education without schools is not new and its accompanying dislike of contrived experiences often extends to specific areas of study. The same criticisms leveled at schools have been directed at the study of communication. The first speech communication departments opened in the early twentieth century and immediately faced opposition from those who found the curriculum superficial.[14] The first generation of speech teachers were accused of cobbling together from other disciplines a course of study that was "dependent and derivative," and of repackaging a commonplace practice—speaking—into an academic specialization that required expertise.[15] Communication classes, critics argued, were redundant, elitist, and trivial.

Communication educators successfully argued the importance of teaching communication skills and by the close of the twentieth century, many college and universities had adopted some version of a communication-across-the-curriculum program.[16] However, while educators no longer struggled to defend the value of communication, the general communication course generated a different problem. It fostered the belief that an education in communication could take the form of generic instruction in a fixed set of basic best practices.[17] The generic curriculum approached sociopolitical complexities with oversimplified principles. Communication competence became a static goal that mistook dominant social norms for universal competence and treated all communicative acts as commensurable.[18]

Educators have sought to reintroduce complexity to the curriculum by foregrounding a key feature of communication: its situated-ness.[19] Situational theories have structured the study of communication since the field's inception. The theories do not align, but they share the belief that communication is context-driven and subject to social norms.[20] A situated approach to communication education fosters the ability to appreciate, navigate, and cultivate different social situations by attending to discursive conventions and local expectations.[21] Such an approach presumes a degree of incommensurability between communicative acts and takes seriously even slight variations in timing, style, arrangement, and delivery. A generic approach might treat such differences as superficial imperfections while a situated approach registers them as possibilities or opportunities to dislodge and modify established discursive patterns.[22] Communication instruction makes space for transformative actions where it does not merely aim to perfect normative practices.[23] Educators committed to making that shift have combined situational theories of communication with theories of situated learning to argue that communication education should be contextualized, stylized for its different audiences, and responsive to the discourse community it serves with competence negotiated locally.[24]

Situated approaches to communication education address the shortcomings of a generic curriculum, but they face an odd dilemma. The approach has led to specialized communication classes tailored to different disciplinary and professional practices. Business students take business communication; engineering students take communication for engineers. While the embedded curriculum aims to account for communication's situated-ness, it often ends up concealing it. When detached from any overarching theory of meaning-making, the situated approach can inadvertently lend local competencies and specialized practices a sense of universality.[25] Students may develop a particular style without an awareness of its contextual limits; they may mistake familiar practices for generalizable principles and presume those practices to be appropriate for every situation. In other words, when communication education is embedded in a specific discourse community, communication's situated-ness, that all-important feature that accounts for communication's mutability, disappears from sight. Students develop communication skills without an awareness of context and miss the chance to experience communication's constitutive power and inventive capacity.

Higher education faces a similar dilemma. The complexity that critics attribute to confusion and dysfunction stems from a situated approach that attracts derision when visible and goes unappreciated when not. Some aspects of that complexity are always visible, such as the differences between campuses—the community colleges, the Ivy Leagues, land grant universities, regional public campuses, and small private liberal arts colleges, each with their own specialized offerings, unusual requirements, unique missions, one-of-a-kind facilities, inconsistent admissions standards, and idiosyncratic bureaucracies. Academia's institutional differences are evident, but the constitutive power and inventive capacity they represent is less apparent. When high education operates without a situational sensibility, without an ability to appreciate, navigate, and cultivate situated approaches, it renders its own complexity a bug rather than a worthwhile feature. When viewed without that sensibility, the differences between campuses appear gratuitous, inefficient, and even dubious, especially to critics like Carey who believe that education is a matter of accessing a stable, established body of knowledge.

This project borrows situated approaches to communication education and mobilizes them for the purposes of educational advocacy. Situated approaches to communication education offer two strategies for responding to anti-school voices and others who cast higher education as lost in an institutional fog. Communication education demonstrates the importance of making situated-ness visible and of viewing situated-ness as a resource rather than a limitation. When communication education takes a situated approach to messaging; when for instance it attends to timing, style, and arrangement, it demonstrates communication's constitutive power.[26] Such an approach emphasizes the iterative and relational dimensions of communication practices.[27] It recognizes the extent to which communication derives power from its own continuous reconstitution, a practice that subjects it to drift and change.[28] The problems with invisibility that embedded lessons generate, that is, the chance that students will mistake the familiar for ideal, illustrate the importance of making visible the contingencies and tailored approaches that shape educational programs. When the structure of a situation disappears from sight, the idea of other possibilities disappears with it. The ability to view situations as constructed fosters a critical capacity, but only if accompanied by appreciation for the possibilities that might emerge from different configurations.

Higher education, like communication, benefits from institutional forms and practices that heighten its visibility. The opportunities to evaluate those forms and practices diminish when they disappear into stale routines or become buried in calcified policies.[29] When instead academics attend to the making and remaking of their institutions, the situated features of that work serve a critical modality. When, for example, Evergreen and CSUMB's founders grappled with water management, faculty housing, and makeshift classroom spaces, they were engaged in reconstituting education, not distracted from it.

Moving education out of schools diminishes our critical capacities by making education harder to see. Anti-school sentiment stems largely from frustration with institutional complexity, but it endures because schools often register as contrived and superficial. Reformers seek something more substantive when they characterize education's artifice as an obstacle to knowledge. However, education without schools mainly renders it invisible, not more genuine. When Cary toured Harvard University, for instance, he found it wrapped in prestige and prone to confusing its own renown for wisdom. He faults the university for mistaking admission to Harvard for an education, and he applauds MIT for avoiding the same mistake. He argues that, by making its classes freely available online, MIT distinguishes the knowledge that it generates from the institution itself. As Carey explains, MIT separates "the quest to understand deep, profound, and beautiful principles of reality" from "the artificial rules and frames of reference that human organizations impose upon us."[30] This arrangement, he concludes, makes MIT the better school because it is the least school-like of the two.

Like reformers before him, Carey argues that education is already everywhere even if educators refuse to recognize its existence outside of schools. Henry A. Giroux made a similar argument when he cautioned academics working at the intersection of cultural studies and critical pedagogy not to limit their work to "what goes on in schools."[31] He proposes that cultural theorists "are remiss in suggesting that pedagogy is primarily about schools and, by implication, that the intersection of cultural studies and pedagogy has little to do with . . . social change outside of traditional sites of schooling."[32] Giroux references Raymond Williams's notion of "permanent education" when he urges us to turn our attention to the "wide ranging set of cultural apparatuses" such as entertainment and consumer practices that serve a pedagogical function.[33] Carey might appreciate Giroux's call to look beyond schools for education, but unlike Giroux, he would have us leverage those other social forces to realize a ubiquitous, always-available form of education. Carey (like Will Hunting) sees institutional activity as needless interference into educational processes. His solution to student debt and limited capacity is to unbundle education from college and meld it with other social processes such as job training or personal pursuits. His is the permanent education that Williams warned against. These non-school apparatuses, Williams explained, become embedded in social life and form "the educational force of our whole social and cultural experience."[34] Where Giroux raised alarm over uneven distributions of power and representation in non-school spheres, Williams saw a different problem. These educational forces are dangerous, he argued, because *we do not see them as education at all.* These embedded, invisible forms of education appear instead as benign socialization, the natural order of things, market forces, or mere life experience. Williams warned that the precepts and trajectories of invisible forms of education cannot be questioned because we cannot critique social structures that we cannot see. His argument offers one simple reason to have schools: they keep education visible. Schools serve a critical function by enabling the evaluation of accepted educational forms against other possibilities. It would be difficult, for instance, for Carey to critique practices like those he observed at Harvard were we to "unbundle" higher education from its institutions and replace colleges and universities with one ubiquitous University of Everywhere. Carey himself was able to advance his criticisms of Harvard only because we register Harvard as an educational project. Elitism would not disappear were college campuses to close, but it would be much harder to critique its non-institutional forms.

Williams gives reason to maintain educational visibility, but greater visibility alone will not endear critics to schools. Concerned that educators take traditional forms for granted, A. Bartlett Giamatti warned against an institutional hubris "that believes the institution's value is so self-evident that it no longer needs explication, its mission so manifest that it no longer requires definition and articulation."[35] Cary's prejudice against institutional artifice signals the twin challenges educational advocates face: how to show the administrative details of colleges and universities as inventive rather than capricious or confused? How, in other words, to invite critics to view schools with a situational sensibility? A less prominent line of educational advocacy offers a preliminary answer that defends complexity as a worthwhile feature.

In 1980, the Carnegie Council on Policy Studies in Higher Education published a report that cast complexity as an achievement.[36] *Three Thousand Futures: The Next Twenty Years for Higher Education* responded to that era's educational polemics, including Heller, Fashing and Deutsch. The Council found no merit in the claim that higher education was experiencing a "crisis" and they instead characterized the 1970s as marked more by transformation than decline.[37] Ninety-five percent of all campuses, they explained, had undergone significant change in enrollments, mergers, oversight, affiliation, or classification. New schools opened and some closed. As the Council described it, higher education had no status quo in the 1970s. Colleges and universities "moved up and down, in and out, and sideways," inviting "3,000 different futures."[38] They cautioned against underestimating American higher education and its "boundless variety among and within institutions."[39] That variety, they concluded, "is a great national resource."[40]

When reformers call for reductions in higher education's bulk and freedom from its bureaucracy, advocates would do well to revive the Council's argument. When reformers demand that academia resolve or eliminate its complexity, colleges and universities might instead aim to heighten it by presenting their work as localized in practice, limited in reach, grounded in sociopolitical histories, and always a work in progress. When education's situated-ness becomes academia's heterogeneity it appears as a means of securing multiple and distinctive vantage points from which to view education and knowledge production. What critics characterize as a flaw serves instead to foster a critical modality. Richard Nichols modeled that modality when he pointed to the forested peninsula to show "what really makes Evergreen as a campus Evergreen." Marsha Moroh likewise modeled it when she characterized the repurposed army housing as "a living learning community." Neither assumed that we would see a college in a patch of forest or a university in a collection of houses. Theirs were declarative, constitutive statements that gave shape to new sites of education and conditions for academic work. Their statements might seem especially significant in that they contributed to founding new campuses, but inventive action in education is not exclusive to founding moments. As the Council explains, colleges and universities continuously reconstitute education through the detailed often repetitive administrative work that follows after the founding.

The Council's defense of three thousand different futures is exceptional in educational literature. Other studies defend education's situated-ness, but not the inventiveness that flows from it, and a defense of situated-ness alone empties the concept of its critical force. Martha C. Nussbaum's national survey of philosophy programs, for instance, grapples with the question of whether widening differences between campuses jeopardizes the prospect of a well-rounded liberal arts education. With all its specialized areas of study and tailored offerings, does institutional diversity not on some level threaten shared goals? Nussbaum argues that it does not, but only because she sees an educational landscape in which individual campuses offer different routes to the same well-rounded critical mind. For Nussbaum, the beauty of that landscape lies in how each school realizes the same philosophical project. Colleges and universities are not interchangeable, she argues.[41] But she nevertheless finds evidence at each campus of a critical and philosophically infused examination of one's own beliefs or a Socratic education. Nussbaum argues that such an education is both "for every human being" and must be concerned "with the actual situation of the student."[42] To demonstrate how that balance works in practice, she toured dozens of campuses including a private liberal arts college in Nashville, an Ivy League, a California State University campus, and a Catholic university. Each campus, she argues, cultivates both a sense of shared humanity and individuality by attending to the character of the student body and the composition of the institution. Socratic education at a mid-sized, semivocational university thus looks very different than it does at a research institution that hosts a top-ranked philosophy department. One might have a single philosophy requirement and a handful of courses that satisfy it. The other may have multiple philosophy requirements augmented by a robust list of related electives. For Nussbaum, the situated work of individual academics is the same philosophical project realized in miniature. While education looks different from place to place, and everyone goes about it in different ways, all achieve the same goal of helping individuals acquire good habits of mind capable of grappling with complex social issues and finding shared solutions. Nussbaum's argument connects all of higher education with a common thread.[43] She concludes that the differences she finds between schools are not of critical importance. A broad commitment to democratic citizenship connects the general to the particular in education. That belief rests, Janet M. Atwill explains, on the humanist ideal that an education in philosophy produces a subject who "both embodies and transcends the values of a specific cultural milieu."[44] Though Nussbaum advocates that belief through a study of "the concrete situations of the teachers," she credits the bulk of its educational value to broader commitments.[45]

Arguing from a different theoretical lens, Stanley Fish likewise defends higher education's situated-ness and similarly evacuates it of its critical force. Fish draws on a rhetorical tradition that dates back to the Greek sophists to affirm the ways in which colleges and universities arrange their affairs according to professional conventions of their own making. If higher education seems arbitrary and superficial, he argues, the problem is not with the institution. Rather, the problem lies in the distrust of contrived practices, the same distrust often directed at rhetoric. Institutionalization does not compromise the world-as-it-is so much as animates it with its own peculiar, internal logics. As Fish explains, it is "a condition of human life always to be operating as an extension of beliefs and assumptions that are historically contingent," or according to the partial truths that humans fashion in and from situations of our own making.[46] Where we can see those institutional contingencies at work—when they are visible to us—academia is subject to what Fish calls the "hostilities" traditionally leveled at rhetoric.[47] His belief in an inherent rhetorical dimension to all human affairs leads him to characterize the search for artifice-free education as futile. Dispersing higher education into other social spheres, he argues, will only strip it of its professional standing, not generate a more genuine intellectual experience.[48] Moreover, such an organizational approach would put academia in service to the ambitions of other institutions.[49] We trivialize academic convention, he warns, at the peril of education itself.

Fish presents the situated-ness of higher education as a condition of human life that we deny at the risk of philosophical conceit. The same rhetorical force that works in and through higher education, he argues, works in and through all other social affairs. Like any other institution, he explains, higher education will be embedded in professional assumptions of some kind, no matter how we organize it. The only question then for Fish is whether we will acknowledge education's situated-ness or continue the reckless pursuit of education without artifice.

When presented in those terms, situated-ness becomes an unremarkable truism that generates little counterforce against the efforts to overcome it. Fish defends academia as an institution, but gives little sense of what schools accomplish that other institutions do not. Jean Lave provides a better sense of what is at stake in defending schools. We fail to appreciate education's situated-ness, she explains, because of a tendency to associate "situated" with "limited." Even though it too is situated, she explains, we often herald formal education as an achievement in universal excellence rather than a privileged practice. Formal education is thought to be superior because it deals with generalizable cognitive skills that can be transferred from situation to situation. In a comparative study of formal and informal educational practices,

Lave troubles the assumption that only informal or non-institutional forms of education, such as learning to sew a pair of pants, are embedded in social processes and thus are "sticky," "contextually limited," and non-transferable.[50] By that argument, the university, the pinnacle of formal education and arbiter of enduring knowledge, sets the standard for educational excellence. Lave challenges that view, arguing that "there are no exceptions to the situated character of social practice, most especially not schooling."[51] Like Fish, Lave presents the situated-ness of education as a condition that we deny at the risk of ethnocentric hubris. Accepting education's situated-ness, she argues, would transform scholarship from a rigid search for knowledge into a continuous critical practice capable of grappling with the impermanence of our own scholarly insights. Though Lave is interested in how situated-ness serves a critical ethic, she does not propose how academic institutions might foster such a perspective in ways that informal instructional practices do not.

Nussbaum, Fish, and Lave all recognize the situated-ness of education, but each treat it mainly as a condition that must be navigated rather than a feature on which to draw. To say that education is situated is to acknowledge the sociopolitical parameters of any educational project. It does not tell us why those conditions matter. To acknowledge, as Fish does, that colleges and universities are beholden to professional norms does not begin to convey the achievements in academia's expansive, convoluted infrastructures. Beyond being merely situated, colleges and universities also have what Bill Readings characterizes as an institutional weight that "exceeds the beliefs of [its] clientele."[52] The more established they become, the more durable colleges and universities appear, but they must constantly regenerate themselves to retain that sense of durability.[53] That regeneration process always risks looking pedantic, redundant, expensive, and bureaucratic. The localized work of teaching and research amasses few grand accomplishments. Inquiries stretch indefinitely into finer specialized detail. Classes end and begin anew. Policies are implemented and dismantled. Higher education lurches along animated as much by degree requirements and financial aid restrictions as any quest for wisdom. These inexact, indeterminate institutional cycles can be maddening, but they sustain critical practice by acknowledging other possibilities. Higher education is clumsy and cumbersome, but its institutional weight is a critical modality insofar as it demands continuous remaking.

Higher education's artifice is its critical force. To invest in the fragmented, inconsistent, incommensurable campuses that currently dot the landscape is to reinforce its critical capacities. That heterogeneous system sustains discussion of why we engage in education, what we count as knowledge, how we classify it, access it, and its significance to our lives. It issues a standing invitation to invent. It is a historical achievement that began in part with the nineteenth-century Morrill Acts. That legislation launched a movement that saw over two hundred institutions and twenty-four university systems built across fifty states and U.S. territories in less than two hundred years.[54] Christopher Jencks and David Riesman attribute the initial growth of colleges and universities in the U.S. to geographic isolation.[55] Dissatisfied by the need to travel for college, states and cities "set up their own institutions 'responsive to local conditions'" and "involved sectarian, ethnic, and economic differences in viewpoint."[56] Higher education thus emerged first in "a Balkanized pattern that made even the decentralized and polycentric German approach look orderly and monolithic."[57] To the extent that new campuses continue to open and existing ones revise and remodel, that historic project remains unfinished. Each campus contributes to the project by offering a different set of conditions for teaching and inquiry.

This project looks at how to heighten the visibility of those details and advocate their value. I do so through an ethnographic and archival study of two relatively young regional public campuses: Evergreen and CSUMB. Evergreen opened in 1971 and CSUMB in 1995. When I first began this project, I requested permission to conduct research at four different campuses. I eventually focused on Evergreen and CSUMB in part because I had a connection to them. CSUMB is a member of the same twenty-three campus system as my home institution and I earned my bachelor's degree from Evergreen. Those connections afforded me just enough familiarity to speak with members of the faculty about our shared commitments to higher education and our concerns for its future.[58] I interviewed twenty-five faculty Evergreen and CSUMB faculty in all and had informal conversations with that many again. Most of the interviews were conducted in person. One took place in a garden, one at Berkeley (where the person had a winter residency), and another over dinner between classes. People gave me campus tours and walked me between offices to meet their colleagues. Over the course of two years I spoke with lecturers, permanent, and retired faculty. I spoke with deans, a former provost, and a president. I visited with staff, lunched with students, and sat in on a range of classes, meetings, and events. I supplemented this fieldwork with archival research that draws on course catalogs, syllabi, founding documents, and internal memos.

While I admire many of the institutional practices that CSUMB and Evergreen have embraced, this project should not be read as an endorsement of their models. Neither should the details that I share from those campuses be taken as a measure of their success. Beyond my initial sense of connection, Evergreen and CSUMB helped me to realize this project for two reasons: First, their differences stand out more than most; they are unusual enough that it is easier to see in them the inventive and contested practices that structure all of higher education. They lend visibility to the situational considerations that more conventional policies and professional practices obscure. Second, the act of founding a college or university requires extensive description and explanation of academic work; it also requires exceptional levels of ingenuity when it happens with few resources. Evergreen and CSUMB offer many examples of faculty who have both refashioned academic commonplaces and reflected on their work. The examples I present give a sense of how educational advocacy might look if animated by attention to circumstance and appreciation for design constraints.

The unusual features of each campus lent themselves to this project, but the situational sensibility they illustrate comes from the thicker, less scripted descriptions of academic life that I was able to assemble. In the chapters that follow, I highlight the ways in which both have established themselves as alternative schools without becoming alternatives to school and how each have explained and defended their choices since their founding. That advocacy work, along with their relative youth, regionalism, and unusual programming, make it easier to see the thinking behind their respective designs. Their heightened visibility in turn makes it easier to see how the designs of more established and conventional schools are anything but inevitable or indisputable. Evergreen and CSUMB have been responsive to the concern that higher education is too isolated. They have moved "beyond the classroom" by dissolving the traditional boundaries between campuses and surrounding communities. They nevertheless remain well-defined schools with a particular style and approach to education. That combination of alternative programming and a high degree of institutional visibility invites critical reflection on education. Both, for instance, have challenged the normative and discriminatory scripts that underwrite "academic excellence" and exclude many students from inquiry processes. When CSUMB opened, for example, it promised to serve California and "especially the working class and historically undereducated and low-income populations . . . in the immediate Tri-County region."[59] Such a mission could seem modest compared to other California universities, some of which are renowned as world-class. Yet, in choosing to serve a specific region, CSUMB made visible a deficiency in the state's educational system. When the campus was still an idea, the California legislature was in the process of documenting how the state's master plan for higher education had systematically excluded low-income, place-bound populations, particularly Latinx and African American residents. CSUMB helped to alter those trends by building a university for people living in California's central coast. However, the university did more than extend access to a particular region; it expanded access to higher education by constituting a new student population and it did so by presuming that local residents were college-ready, an idea that other educators had long resisted.

The details from Evergreen and CSUMB that I share offer a counternarrative to the quest for ubiquitous, permanent forms of education, such as the University of Everywhere, that promise to render education indistinguishable from the other social spheres to which it might attach. I begin that narrative by illustrating how educators have embraced situated-ness and turned it into an instructional resource. Chapter 1 chronicles Evergreen's efforts to distinguish its educational approach from free-form autodidacticism. The college's reputation for structure-less classes generated the need in the 1970s to show the institution as consequential. Faculty did so by writing extensive course descriptions that detailed the manufactured situations they planned for students. Those descriptions shifted the debate from a question of "structure versus free-form" to a matter of how best to manage the continuous work of arranging and remaking education. It was an approach that reflected a *kairotic* sense of time. Faculty conceptualized their courses as happenings that temporarily coordinated events before self-destructing, a process that required them to remake the curriculum from scratch each year.

Chapter 2 demonstrates that institutional inventiveness is not confined to founding events. It relays how five CSUMB and Evergreen faculty developed specific programs and resources for their campuses and the generative role that personal and professional circumstance played in each case. Faculty constructed educational materials, including community partnerships, unusual classes, and a campus building, by navigating makeshift routes and seizing local, one-off opportunities that all but disappeared behind them. Their work resulted in singular offerings that would be impossible to replicate. In each case, faculty exhibited the qualities of *mêtis*, a type of knowledge suited to complex, shifting, and non-repeatable environments.

The inventiveness that Evergreen and CSUMB exhibit is not unique to those campuses or a feature exclusive to "experimental" or "alternative" education. Chapter 3 contextualizes Evergreen and CSUMB within a larger historical project that spans generations of academic institutions. The first American college boom in the nineteenth century saw the nation's colleges and universities also experimenting with organizational form. Three distinct approaches to education and inquiry exemplify the inventiveness of those efforts: the course elective adopted at Harvard, the Wisconsin Idea developed at the University of Wisconsin (UW), and the rigorous research expectations pioneered at Clark University. The first iterations of these ideas show their arbitrary beginnings and illustrate the long tradition of institutional diversity that has expanded higher education's field of vision. Enshrined in each is the counterintuitive belief that schools generate educational possibilities by placing parameters on endless options. The initial proponents of those ideas, Charles W. Elliot, president of Harvard, John Bascom, president of UW, and G. Stanley Hall, president of Clark, all spoke of the need to manage the possibilities that academia presented by imposing order on education and inquiry. Yet the enduring popularity of their ideas has not curtailed the possibilities that academia courts. Their influence reverberates throughout higher education as illustrated by the threads of those projects visible in CSUMB's Service Learning Institute and Evergreen's Native Pathways Program and Native American and World Indigenous Peoples Studies. Each iteration unsettles and modifies the original with an eye to transforming education.

Despite a long tradition of institutional diversity in U.S. higher education, some policies and practices diminish academia's critical capacities. Chapter 4 offers one such example. It traces the history of credit transfer and the Donahoe Higher Education Act otherwise known as California's Master Plan for Higher Education. Designed primarily to facilitate mobility, credit transfer and articulation policies instead foster the impression that schools are interchangeable and that educational content can exist independent of its institutional form. California's master plan, which is organized around the idea of differentiation of function, deepens that impression by smoothing out or suppressing the differences between individual campuses. Credit transfer was the administrative mechanism that enabled coordination between three systems with differentiated functions. The plan, like Carey's University of Everywhere, is meant to facilitate access, but it discourages inventive practices by assigning each system its own domain and restricting the kinds of academic programs each campus can feature. The history of its organizational structure shows policymakers struggling to define and maintain those domains at the expense of diversified sites of education. When CSUMB first opened, for example, it refused to be constrained by the Master Plan and struggled against the assumptions used to justify the state's policies. It succeeded to a limited extent, but its more radical proposals did not survive the campus's integration into the California system.

California's master plan serves as a cautionary tale for educational reforms that acquiesce to anti-school sentiments. It demonstrates why simply reducing higher education's infrastructure will not improve educational experiences. The concluding chapter looks at two different approaches to reform that both rest on the belief that additional infrastructure obstructs education's central purpose. These approaches to reform encourage us to evaluate individual campuses against an ideal form and to designate institutions as either successes or failures. While each approach intends to better realize their ideals, both risk restricting the scope and reach of the academic project by reducing its visibility and making it harder to evaluate and modify educational conditions. In my final remarks, I return to Evergreen to illustrate what reform efforts might look like were they guided by a situational sensibility. When viewed from that perspective, campuses appear as provisional responses to reoccurring questions rather than better and worse variations on a single model. Their localized forms no longer look like institutional faults and appear instead as inventive contributions to an unfolding project.

NOTES

1. Dick Nichols, "A History of Evergreen from Newspaper Headlines," Pack Forest Faculty Retreat, 1972. Video edited by D.F. Smith. The Evergreen Visual History Collection, Malcolm Stilson Archives and Special Collections, The Evergreen State College, Olympia, WA: http://blogs.evergreen.edu/visualhistory/?p=568.

2. Ibid.

3. Ibid.

4. Sharon S. Goldsmith, "Beyond Restructuring: Building a University for the 21st Century," Paper presented for the Annual Meeting of the Association for the Study of Higher Education (Orland, FL: November 3, 1995), 18–19.

5. Marsha Moroh (Dean of CSU Monterey Bay's College of Science, Media Arts and Technology) in conversation with the author (Seaside, CA: March 13, 2013).

6. Ibid.

7. Kevin Carey, *The End of College: Creating the Future of Learning and the University of Everywhere* (New York: Riverhead Books, 2016).

8. Anya Kamenetz, *DIY U: Edupunks, Edupreneurs, and the Coming Transformation of Higher Education* (Hartford, VT: Chelsea Green Publishing, 2010); Richard A. DeMillo and A. J. Young, *Revolution in Higher Education: How a Small Band of Innovators Will Make College Accessible and Affordable* (Boston, MA: MIT Press, 2015).

9. Will's famous quote sums up his attitude toward school: "the sad thing about a guy like you is, in fifty years, you're going to start doing some thinking on your own and you're going to come up with the fact that . . . you dropped a hundred and fifty grand on a fucking education you could have got for a dollar fifty in late charges at the public library."

10. Jean-Jacques Rousseau, *Emile, or On Education*, trans., Allan Bloom (New York: Basic Books, 1979); Friedrich Nietzsche, *On the Future of Our Educational Institutions* (South Bend, IN: St. Augustine's Press, 2004); Henry David Thoreau, *Walden, or Life in the Woods* (Boston, MA: Ticknor and Fields, 1854); Thorstein Veblen, *The Higher Learning in America: A Memorandum on the Conduct of Universities by Business Men* (New York: B.W. Huebsch, 1918); A. S. Neill, *Summerhill: A Radical Approach to Child Rearing* (New York: Hart Publishing Co, 1960).

11. Joseph Fashing and Steven E. Deutsch, *Academics in Retreat: the Politics of Educational Innovation* (Albuquerque: University of New Mexico Press, 1971), 276.

12. Louis G. Heller, *The Death of the American University: With Special Reference to the Collapse of City College of New York* (New Rochelle, NY: Arlington House, 1973), 64.

13. Fashing and Deutsch, *Academics*, 13; Heller, *Death*, 196.

14. Gerry Philipsen, "Paying Lip Service to 'Speech' in Disciplinary Naming, 1914–1954," *A Century of Communication Studies: The Unfinished Conversation*, Eds. William M. Keith and Pat J. Gehrke (New York: Routledge, 2014): 58–75.

15. Herman Cohen, *The History of Speech Communication: The Emergence of a Discipline, 1914–1945* (Annandale, VA: Speech Communication Association, 1995), 43.

16. Sherwyn P. Morreale, Pamela Shockley-Zalabak, Penny Whitney, "The Center for Excellence in Oral Communication: Integrating Communication Across the Curriculum," *Communication Education 42*, no. 1 (1993): 10–21; Sherwyn Morreale, "Communication Across the Curriculum and in Undergraduate Education Debated and Clarified," *Spectra 33*, no. 4 (1997): 5–14; Sherwyn P. Morreale, Michael M. Osborn, and Judy C. Pearson, "Why Communication Is Important: A Rationale for the Centrality of the Study of Communication," *JACA-ANNANDALE-* 1 (2000): 1–25.

17. Deanna P. Dannels, "Time to Speak Up: A Theoretical Framework of Situated Pedagogy and Practice for Communication Across the Curriculum," *Communication Education* 50, no. 2 (2001): 144–158; Colleen Garside, "Seeing the Forest through the Trees: A Challenge Facing Communication Across the Curriculum Programs," *Communication Education* 51, no. 1 (2001): 51–64.

18. Jo Sprague, "Retrieving the Research Agenda for Communication Education: Asking the Pedagogical Questions That Are 'Embarrassments to Theory,'" *Communication Education* 42, no. (1993): 106–122; Deanna P. Dannels, "Leaning In and Letting Go," *Communication*

Education 54, no. 1 (2005): 1–5; Deanna P. Dannels, "Communication Across the Curriculum Problematics and Possibilities: Standing at the Forefront of Educational Reform," *The Sage Handbook of Communication and Instruction*, Eds. Deanna L. Fassett & John T. Warren (Thousand Oaks, CA: Sage, 2010), 55–79.

19. Dannels, "Time to Speak Up"; Dannels, "Leaning In and Letting Go."

20. Mary Yost, "Training Four Minute Men at Vassar," *Quarterly Journal of Speech Education* 5, no. 3 (1919): 246–253; Lloyd F. Bitzer, "The Rhetorical Situation," *Philosophy & Rhetoric* 1, no. 1 (1968): 1–14; Richard E. Vatz, "The Myth of the Rhetorical Situation," *Philosophy & Rhetoric* 6, no. 3 (1973): 154–161; Michael Burgoon, Judee K. Heston, and James C. McCroskey, "The Small Group as a Unique Communication Situation," *Messages: A Reader in Human Communication*, Ed. J.M. Civikly (New York: Random House, 1977), 158–166; Barbara A. Biesecker, "Rethinking the Rhetorical Situation from Within the Thematic of 'Différance'," *Philosophy & Rhetoric* 22, no. 2 (1989): 110–130.

21. Pat J. Gehrke, "Paladins, Mercenaries, and Practicable Pedagogy," *Communication and Critical/Cultural Studies* 6, no. 4 (2009): 416–420; Troy A. Murphy, "Deliberative Civic Education and Civil Society: A Consideration of Ideals and Actualities in Democracy and Communication Education," *Communication Education* 53, no. 1 (2004); Troy B. Cooper, "The Impromptu Rhetorical Situation," *Communication Teacher* 33, no. 4 (2019): 262–265; Jessy J. Ohl, "Reinvigorating Civic Education in Communication Through *Imitatio*," *Communication Teacher* (2020): 1–5.

22. John Durham Peters, *Speaking into the Air: A History of the Idea of Communication* (Chicago: University of Chicago Press, 1999); John Muckelbauer, *The Future of Invention: Rhetoric, Postmodernism, and the Problem of Change* (Albany: State University of New York Press, 2008).

23. For extended discussions of the implications of that distinction see: Barbara Biesecker, *Addressing Postmodernity: Kenneth Burke, Rhetoric, and a Theory of Social Change* (University of Alabama Press, 2000) and Karma R. Chávez, *Queer Migration Politics: Activist Rhetoric and Coalitional Possibilities* (Carbondale: University of Illinois Press, 2013).

24. John S. Brown, Allan Collins, and Paul Duguid, "Situated Cognition and the Culture of Learning," *Educational Researcher*, 18 (1989): 32–42; Jean Lave, "Situated Learning in Communities of Practice," *Perspectives on Socially Shared Cognition*, Eds. Lauren B. Resnick, John M. Levine, & Stephanie D. Teasley (American Psychological Association, 1991): 63–83; Jean Lave and E. Wenger, *Situated Learning: Legitimate Peripheral Participation* (U.K.: Cambridge University Press, 1991); Dannels, "Time to Speak Up"; Ann L. Darling and Deanna P. Dannels, "Practicing Engineers Talk about the Importance of Talk: A Report on the Role of Oral Communication in the Workplace," *Communication Education* 52, no. 1 (2003): 1–16.

25. Dannels, "Communication Across the Curriculum."

26. For a history of different instructional approaches to the rhetorical canon and rhetoric's shifting position in liberal arts education see: Bruce A. Kimball, *Orators and Philosophers: A History of the Idea of Liberal Education* (New York: College Board, 1995); Richard A. Lanham, *The Electronic Word: Democracy, Technology, and the Arts* (Chicago: University of Chicago Press, 1995); Sharon Crowley, "Of Gorgias and Grammatology," *College Composition and Communication* 30 (1979): 279–283; Robert Craig, "Communication," *Encyclopedia of Rhetoric*, Ed. Thomas O. Sloane (Oxford University Press, 2001), 125–37; Michael MacDonald, "Encomium of Hegel," *Philosophy & Rhetoric* 39, no. 1 (2006): 22–44.

27. Karen Burke LeFevre, *Invention as a Social Act* (Carbondale: Southern Illinois University Press, 1987); Janet M. Atwill and Janice M. Lauer, Eds. *Perspectives on Rhetorical Invention* (Knoxville: University of Tennessee Press, 2002); Peter Simonson, "Reinventing Invention, Again," *Rhetoric Society Quarterly* 44, no. 4 (2014): 299–322.

28. Kenneth Burke, *A Rhetoric of Motives* (Berkeley: University of California Press, 1950), 26; Muckelbauer, *Future of Invention*. Kenneth Burke suggests rhetoric is most powerful as "a general *body of identifications* that owe their convincingness much more to trivial repetition and dull daily reënforcement than to exceptional rhetorical skill" (emphasis and spelling original). Rhetoric's dependence on repetition ensures its instability.

29. Sara Ahmed, *On Being Included: Racism and Diversity in Institutional Life* (Durham, NC: Duke University Press, 2012). Ahmed makes this same point through a review of "new institutionalism" and phenomenology.

30. Carey, *The End of College*, 169.

31. Henry A. Giroux, "Cultural Studies, Public Pedagogy, and the Responsibility of Intellectuals," *Communication and Critical/Cultural Studies* 1, no. 1 (2004): 60.

32. Ibid., 61.

33. Ibid., 63.

34. Raymond Williams, *Communications* (New York: Penguin Books 1962), 14.

35. A. Bartlett Giamatti, *A Free and Ordered Space: The Real World of the University* (New York: W.W. Norton & Company, 1988), 25.

36. Carnegie Council on Policy Studies in Higher Education. *Three Thousand Futures: The Next Twenty Years for Higher Education* (San Francisco, CA: Jossey-Bass, 1980); John A. Douglass, "The Carnegie Commission and Council on Higher Education: A Retrospective" (Berkeley, CA: Center for Studies in Higher Education, 2005). The Council was the research arm of the Carnegie Corporation established in 1967 under the direction of Clark Kerr.

37. Fashing and Deutsch, *Academics*, xix.

38. Carnegie Council, *Three Thousand Futures,* 79.

39. Ibid., 135.

40. Ibid., 136.

41. Martha C. Nussbaum, *Cultivating Humanity: A Classical Defense of Reform in Liberal Education* (Cambridge, MA: Harvard University Press, 1997), 6.

42. Ibid., 31–32.

43. Janet M. Atwill, *Rhetoric Reclaimed: Aristotle and the Liberal Arts Tradition* (Ithaca, NY: Cornell University Press, 1998), 41. Nussbaum's argument is representative of a historical trend in the humanities and liberal arts curriculum that Janet M. Atwill traces. That trend, she argues, is organized around a commitment to "reproducing normative subjects and normative bodies of knowledge."

44. Atwill, *Rhetoric Reclaimed*, 23.

45. Nussbaum, *Cultivating Humanity*, 6.

46. Stanley Fish, *Doing What Comes Naturally: Change, Rhetoric, and the Practice of Theory in Literary and Legal Studies* (Durham: Duke University Press, 1989), 246.

47. Ibid., 219.

48. Stanley Fish, *Save the World on Your Own Time* (London: Oxford University Press, 2012).

49. Immanuel Kant, *The Conflict of the Faculties*, trans, Mary J. Gregor (University of Nebraska Press, 1992). Fish borrows this argument from Immanuel Kant who advanced it in his treatise *The Conflict of the Faculties*.

50. Jean Lave, *Apprenticeship in Critical Ethnographic Practice* (Chicago: The University of Chicago Press, 2011), 18.

51. Lave, *Apprenticeship*, 19.

52. Bill Readings, *The University in Ruins* (Cambridge, MA: Harvard University Press, 1996), 171.

53. Jacques Derrida, *Who's Afraid of Philosophy?; Right to Philosophy I*, Trans. Jan Plug (Stanford, CA: Stanford University Press, 2002), 10. Jacques Derrida notes how the "apparent firmness, hardness, durability, or resistance of philosophical institutions betrays, first of all, the fragility of a foundation."

54. The exclusion of Blacks and African American people from public universities was a part of the conditions established by the Morrill Acts, a historical detail that illustrates the importance of keeping educational conditions visible and thus available for critique.

55. Chrisopher Jencks and David Riesman, *The Academic Revolution* (Garden City, NY: Doubleday, 1968).

56. Ibid., 155, 158.

57. Ibid., 157.

58. Sara L. McKinnon, Robert Asen, Karma R. Chávez, and Robert Glenn Howard, *text +
FIELD: Innovations in Rhetorical Method* (University Park: Pennsylvania University Press,
2016). My ethnographic work follows a turn within rhetorical studies toward field methods.

59. "California State University, Monterey Bay Vision Statement" (Seaside, CA: September
27, 1994).

Chapter One

Something Will Be Happening

Washington's state legislature never mentioned alternative education when it approved a new regional college in 1967. Their objective was to increase the state's enrollment capacity and meet the growing demand for post-secondary education. Those considerations drove the decision to choose Thurston County, the state's most underserved region, as the home for Washington's newest college. Geography was the college's first defining feature and its location inspired the first visions of the college. Advocates imagined a campus integrated with the state capital in Olympia and enriched by the surrounded mountains and water. When Garrett Heyns, President of the Southwestern Washington State College Committee, addressed both chambers of the legislature on the eve of their vote, he spoke of a "happy union of capital and college campuses."[1] He suggested that state facilities might serve as "'laboratories'" in government where students could gain practical experience.[2] He touted the access that students would enjoy to the Pacific Ocean and Mount Rainer. A description of the college issued by its planners in 1970 promoted the same local features, noting its "nearness to state government" and its "large tree-covered and water-oriented campus" which would be used "as a living laboratory for a variety of inquiries."[3] The vision of a college animated by its locality lent some definition to an institution that for several years existed only on paper.

After the college was approved, it began to attract hope for a new kind of educational institution. The first mention of an alternative college came from the state's council of university presidents who proposed a diverse system of public institutions capable of serving a range of individual talents and interests.[4] Legislators from around the state caught the vision. Senator Gordon Sandison of Port Angeles attended the Board of Trustees' first meeting and advised against replicating the traditional college model. "It was not the intent of the Legislature," he shared, "that this be just another four-year college . . . bound by any rigid structure of tradition."[5] James E. Brooks, President of Central Washington State College, also advised the trustees to consider alternative institutional designs.[6] He gifted them with copies of a recent study by Allen J. Brumbaugh who advocated flexibility and a capacity for "continuous revision."[7] A new college "oriented to the present and the future," Brumbaugh cautioned, "cannot afford to replicate a program that harks back to earlier times, no matter how outstanding it may have been."[8] Brumbaugh provided examples of colleges that had dispensed with grades and course requirements and were experimenting with interdisciplinary classes, student-designed curriculum, and the inclusion of under-studied or previously ignored subject areas.[9] The trustees, perhaps overwhelmed at the possibilities, elected to leave educational philosophy to its appointees to whom they extended an invitation to experiment. The faculty did not start entirely from scratch when they accepted that invitation. They adopted the two themes that thus far defined the college: "place" and "flexibility." Those twin commitments formed the basis of the educational model that gradually developed at The Evergreen State College. They appear in the college's 1972–1973 catalog, which speaks about Evergreen's intention to graduate "effective learners" able to "cope more flexibly and confidently with a world very much in flux."[10]

This chapter does not take up the question of whether Evergreen succeeded in its goal to produce more effective learners. It follows instead the discussion that occurred in the college's early years about the value of designating a formal time and place for education. Though sometimes associated with anti-school movements, Evergreen is a study in careful educational administration. The college rejected the traditional model of stable departments and course offerings and instead embraced continuous reinvention of curricular domains. The faculty, resistant to the idea that courses were mere content vehicles for knowledge, conceptualized their classes as *happenings*, or a combination of planned activity and chance convergence that must be re-made again each academic year. While regionalism influenced the campus as its first planners had hoped, the faculty also forged unique educational places from their collective expertise and student interests. The combination of singular happenings and localized lessons made visible—and vivid—the continuous planning and arranging that distinguishes formal education from the informal learning that is a routine matter of human affairs.

Curricular flexibility and regional commitments are not unique to Evergreen. The college is a noteworthy exemplar for a different reason: its unusual curricular design brings heightened visibility to the situated quality of education. Of note here is not the specific pedagogical model that Evergreen developed but the constitutive and inventive role that institutional processes play in educational design. Evergreen's processes illuminate the situational aspects of academic work that can be difficult to see at other institutions. That visibility serves as a reminder that nothing is inevitable or certain about education, even in institutions that follow convention. This chapter documents the situational sensibility that Evergreen faculty brought to their work through a close reading of the college's 1971 inaugural course catalog and the "program histories" that faculty published for each of their courses. It offers a vivid account of the continuous planning and arranging underway at the campus with particular focus on the circumstantial judgments that shape all instruction but that remain invisible in more traditional course catalogs and syllabi.[11]

The Difference between No Structure and Alternative Structure

Planning for the new college began in earnest in 1967 amidst a national conversation then underway about the need for new models of education. Between 1960 and 1972, some four hundred experimental or "free schools"—grade school, high school, and college level—opened across the country.[12] Free schools popularized the belief that education should be less disciplined, less concerned with information-acquisition, and more about engagement with the world at large. In their effort to move away from rote instruction and indoctrination, free school advocates sought less cloistered, more holistic forms of education that merged formal with informal learning processes and unyoked schools from the bridle of tradition. In lieu of the traditional quest for universal knowledge, free schools, many of which operated out of makeshift spaces, improvised curriculum in response to student interests and immediate environments.[13] Troubled by what Ivan Illich called the "custodial care" or dependency that traditional schooling fostered in students, free school advocates looked to the students themselves as reliable sources of their own education.[14] The free school movement in general espoused flexibility and the belief that life itself offered the best education. For many free schoolers, the materiality and spontaneity of the everyday, such as the sudden need to repair a bicycle or administer first aid, provided all the structure that a curriculum required.[15]

Free schools played a part in shaping public attitudees toward Evergreen, but post-secondary alternative schools, many of them modeled after Alexander Meiklejohn's 1920s experimental college at the University of Wisconsin, had a more direct influence on Evergreen's curriculum and pedagogy. Alternative programs and colleges that pre-date Evergreen include the General Program Experiment at San Jose State College and its peer project, the Experimental Collegiate Program at University of California, Berkeley (1965–69), Fordham University's Bensalem College (1967–74), Franconia College in New Hampshire (1963–78), State University of New York, Old Westbury (1967 with reorganization in 1971), New College of Florida

(1964–75), and Fairhaven College, which opened in Western Washington State College in 1968. [16] Many of these projects operated within a traditional college or university structure but replaced the textbook-lecture-exam model with interdisciplinary, integrated, independent study. [17] Like the free schools, these college programs also looked to the immediate surroundings for educational inspiration. Franconia's course catalog, for instance, opens with an invitation to see the natural landscape of its campus as a classroom:

> When you stand on the front porch of the college on a clear day, your eye travels out across the Easton Valley and up to Kinsman, Cannon, Franconia Notch, and finally Lafayette which, if you are in condition, you can climb in a day. Or you can walk in the college's 200 acres of forest which serve as a laboratory for those students interested in ecology, geology, mountain climatology, natural history, forestry and conservation. [18]

Franconia designed its curriculum around what it called "core" courses. Students spent two years studying twelve "samples" or "moments" of human experience in which "someone made a very significant decision from which we can learn." [19] In hopes of acquiring general skills through the study of specific problems, students formulated broad questions and ideas while attending to the particulars of a moment. "We find," the college explained of its approach, "that the meaning of decisions becomes ever more complex." [20] Evergreen adopted similar course models including a first year "core" course designed to teach students how to think by studying specific combinations of subject matters.

The unaccredited Black Mountain College, which operated from 1933 to 1957 in rural North Carolina and which also influenced Evergreen's founders, exemplifies another thread of the alternative education movement underway in the mid-twentieth century. While many free schools sought forms of self-expression unhindered by social imposition (and struggled with solipsism), faculty at Black Mountain experimented with concepts like order, contingency, failure, and chance in an effort to rethink the structure of both artistic and educational practice. [21] A number of renowned figures of American modern music, theater, and design taught at Black Mountain including John Cage and Buckminster Fuller. Their landmark theories and principles of design were developed in part while teaching at Black Mountain. Among the precepts that informed their teaching was the idea that loyalty to tradition alienated people from the present and the future; that art has formal and social responsibilities beyond serving as a vehicle for expression; and that design is "process and action" and not "a single object." [22]

The influence of these educational programs on Evergreen is acknowledged in a letter from President Charles J. McCann to Evergreen's first class. He introduced Evergreen as "a learning community that reflects the nature of the real world, where none of the problems man faces is simple and where none of the parts becomes, in its own conception, more important than the whole."[23] McCann used a phrase to describe the new college that his readers might have associated with the free school movement. Evergreen, he explained, "was designed from the outset to operate at times as a 'college without walls.'"[24] While the phrase reflects the college's interest in the non-academic forms of education available beyond the campus, it referred primarily to the college's commitment to dissolving the disciplinary silos that partition traditional campuses into departments and majors. A college without walls, however, was not a college without structure; it was not what John Dewey called "planless improvisation."[25] In an early statement on institutional design, McCann described the kind of structure that the college offered and how it differed from both traditional and other alternative schools. Where traditional academic institutions organized along established divisions, McCann described a college organized around malleable connections. Evergreen, he explained, "stresses cooperation and interchange among members of a learning community, allowing faculty and students to work together in a mutual quest for information and for solutions to real problems."[26]

As McCann explained it, Evergreen's structure enabled collaboration between students and faculty and across areas of study. It would be difficult to forge such connections at a traditional institution that segregated subjects and arranged classes around a single topic. It would be equally difficult, Evergreen's designers suggested, to forge imaginative and unconventional connections on one's own, in the wide-open world, against the weight of established order and without the architectonic structure the college provided. That kind of imaginative, inventive inquiry required resources and facilitation. A 1969 memo from Vice President Edward Joseph Shoben regarding Evergreen's lecture halls exhibits the level of detail that went into designing a campus that could support such work. Shoben expressed his hesitation about a plan for lecture halls that could seat one hundred and fifty students. "I can't escape some worries," he wrote to his colleagues, that the lecture halls "don't seem properly in phase with either our educational aspirations or our economic necessities, and I am unpersuaded that curtain walls and other similar devices would not have enlarged our flexibility."[27] At the faculty Planning Conference held February 8, 1970, Charles B. Teske, Dean of
Humanities and Arts made a similar comment about how best to plan for connection rather than replicate traditional academic divisions. Teske was thinking in this case about how student support services such as computer labs and writing centers fit into the curriculum and he made a case for recognizing the people who staffed those services as part of the faculty. "I see no reason," he said, "why the facilities and service staff of the college should not consider themselves also to be faculty members."[28]

The rapid demise of many free schools foreshadowed the challenges Evergreen would face in actualizing a nontraditional, flexible structure. Its greatest challenge lay in distinguishing its immersive learning environments from an anti-school sentiment in which anything, even "just being," counted as education.[29] In its effort to achieve a balance between open exploration and adherence to a course of study, the college risked moving so far outside the traditional classroom that education appeared indistinguishable from autodidactic, extra-curricular activity. Such a model of education, its critics argued, did not warrant institutional support and some expressed doubt that Evergreen's curriculum contributed in meaningful ways to instructional practices that might have occurred anyway as a matter of social life. Others criticized the campus for being immobilized by a flat hierarchy and a fear of indoctrination. A manifesto that circulated through the campus in the spring of 1972 spoke of an "extreme do-your-own-thingism" that had ahold of the college.[30] Evergreen, they warned, was generating rigidity of a different kind: student inertia. When everything became education and education became anything, learning resembled moving in place.

Though Evergreen presented its campus and the surrounding natural and social environment as a classroom writ large, its curriculum was not life itself. To ensure that the institution not become inconsequential or its influence invisible, the faculty made an effort to articulate nontraditional practices with formal educational activities and traditional academics. Doing so challenged the faculty to reconcile their critiques of academic convention with their investment in the new campus without either diminishing the place of school in education or simply exchanging traditional materials for current topics of the day. In looking for ways to reimagine college and academic professional life, the faculty fashioned the classroom, the syllabus, and the course as pliable building materials. The result was a curriculum grounded in manufactured situations made possible by the structure the college provided.

The Curriculum as Rhythmic Loop

Evergreen's inaugural course catalog and the "program histories" that faculty wrote for each concluded course give a sense of the structuring role the faculty envisioned for the college. Published in January 1971, Evergreen's 1971–1972 catalog set the tenor for the new campus, establishing much of the general policy that would appear in subsequent catalogs. In that first year, the catalog bore the responsibility of explaining the college to its multiple constituencies—prospective students, prospective faculty, parents, the state legislature, and the public—all of whom wanted to know what an alternative college curriculum looked like. In the letter to students that opens the catalog, President McCann explains that it was more of a "prospectus" than a catalog: a proposal of "activities yet to happen."[31] To that end, the 170-page document details how Evergreen would provide an education without majors, requirements, grades, or traditional courses. Not as crowded with administrative information and policies as the catalogs of established colleges, the bulk of the 1971 catalog is dedicated to describing the "coordinated studies programs," the team-taught, year-long courses built around broad interdisciplinary themes that have become Evergreen's hallmark, and "contracted studies," an expanded version of the independent study. In his letter, McCann cautions students not to think of Evergreen as an alternative to school. He acknowledges that some "may be attracted to Evergreen by the absence of some old familiar forms such as GPA's," and he discourages students from thinking of attending the college "merely to escape these superficialities."[32] An explanation of "contract studies" describes them as "something quite different from 'doing your own thing.'"[33] Statements like these addressed common stereotypes of alternative schools, particularly the belief that school simply legitimated the education available in everyday life. While the college invited students to study whatever they might wish, it also invited them to think about why they might wish to do so in the company and guidance of others. "If it is completely 'your own thing' and does not call for experienced, challenging guidance," the catalog advised, "then you can do it much better, much more efficiently, and much more honestly without joining a college which is responsible for offering such guidance."[34] In this the college acknowledged the crux of the debate over traditional education: school was not the only way to acquire an education; it was not even in every case the most practical or expedient way to educate one's self, nor was it always a genuine form of education. Such statements set the stage to consider what else a college might offer other than authorized and credentialed education while the catalog worked to make visible the structure that the college lent to education and inquiry.

In contrast to the catalog, the program histories were internal, less formal documents that gave faculty a chance to reflect on their pedagogy and curricular design. Faculty began the practice of writing program histories at the end of the first academic year and many continued the practice until the early 1990s. The program histories from the 1970s vary in form and length, ranging from a few to twenty pages.[35] Some consist of no more than a syllabus and schedule. Others include course materials and rosters alongside faculty narratives. Some are handwritten. Many include humorous asides, often at the expense of the authors. Of the twenty-eight archived histories written between 1972 and 1978, none of the programs repeat. In keeping with Evergreen's commitment to renew its offerings each year, the histories compile general knowledge, mostly related to pedagogy, and otherwise document one-time course offerings. While the individual programs came to an end, these histories document the significant, modest, and often intangible contributions each made to the college's emerging campus. The unusual form and the absence of academic convention makes it possible to see in them what can be difficult to see in traditional institutions: the collective effort to constitute distinct grounds for education and inquiry.

Both the 1971 course catalog and the program histories show Evergreen faculty enacting a situational sensibility in their work. Co-authored in many cases, these documents share several notable stylistic tendencies that suggest faculty were mining the inventive possibilities of structured education to coordinate happenings and events. As described in the catalog and the program histories, the organization of a course was more consequential than its content. The descriptions include a remarkable amount of detail about course design, in part to explain the value of academics to audiences who may not share an investment in it. Likewise, many of the program histories, written as first person accounts, give less attention to specific content than to activities. While Evergreen faculty took care in choosing specific course materials, the bulk of their energy went toward establishing the time, place, and conditions for education. They hosted events and brought people together. These arrangements imposed parameters on learning and inquiry and did so in such a way that allowed divergent and sometimes unplanned approaches to questions and topics to emerge within a single course. Like their free school counterparts, Evergreen faculty saw educational potential in everything and sought to accommodate the study of virtually any topic. Unlike the free school model that treated structure as an obstacle to realizing the educational potential of everyday life, Evergreen faculty purposefully imposed structure onto instruction and inquiry.

More than it defined itself by any educational philosophy, Evergreen defined itself against the rigidity of traditional institutions that defended conventional academic organization as necessary and ideal. However, Evergreen faculty were not opposed to structure. The uncertainty that Evergreen introduced into its courses came *not* from unstructured learning but from its flexible approach. Evergreen was alternative in the sense that it hosted a curriculum that could be easily re-organized, revised, or re-imagined altogether. In order to maintain flexibility, faculty agreed to allow programs to "self-destruct" at the end of each year and to plan new programs from scratch.[36] They adopted a cohort model of teaching, and left space in the curriculum for student interests. As was true throughout academia, inquiry at Evergreen was coordinated, or what the catalog described as a "cooperative" endeavor.[37] Importantly, the knowledge its courses generated did not take the form of a linear progression of thought; it instead flashed and blinked like a constellation of stars across an ever-changing terrain.

The Time of Education

The course descriptions in Evergreen's inaugural catalog explain the ways in which Evergreen would differ from other colleges and the ways it would resemble them. Apart from a few obvious differences, such as the preference for assigning primary sources rather than textbooks and the opportunities to conduct inquiries alongside faculty, much of the content resembled that found at other campuses. It was expected that Evergreen students would develop their reading and writing skills along with information and quantitative literacy. Faculty invited speakers and planned field trips. They selected materials with a recognizable connection to a given field of study. The program "The Individual, the Citizen, and the State," for instance, included study of the "classics in political theory from Plato to Mao."[38] The program "Communications and Intelligence" involved regular film screenings and scheduled time in the media lab. Though comprised of recognizable elements, the unusual organizational structure of its coordinated programs most distinguished Evergreen's classes from the traditional college course. The programs were envisioned from the outset as one-time offerings. Three to five faculty members worked in teams to design basic and advanced courses that would begin in the fall and continue through the spring when students would complete culminating projects. Similar themes might be revisited in future programs, but, as the catalog explained, faculty would plan altogether different courses each year.

On the one hand the catalog describes a familiar scholastic routine: organized reading, thinking, observing, discussing, and writing. At the same time, faculty exercised their freedom to create unusual pairings, and in doing so, to show the creative power that educational institutions have to structure learning and articulate ideas. The academic life the catalog describes is both rhythmic and uncertain. The balance achieved between those two qualities combined with the willingness to make visible the work of *arranging* a syllabus and *coordinating* studies distinguishes Evergreen's curriculum from other formal and informal educational models.

The structure that Evergreen imposed on learning is most visible where the catalog mentions practices that would be so taken for granted elsewhere as to not warrant mention at all. Such is the case with the description of a yearlong program called "Political Ecology." The catalog description includes a statement so generic that it could be an apt description for virtually any college course. "Once a week," the catalog explains, "all members of the program will meet to hear a lecture related to the current reading assignment, or to see a related film, or perhaps to do both."[39] It goes on to list not only the books the class would read but how and when they would read them: "We shall read thoroughly at least one major book each week and meet twice weekly in small groups to discuss our readings."[40] A similar kind of statement appears in the description of "Communications and Intelligence" that likewise gives a sense of how students might expect to spend their time: "During a typical week, one may attend an afternoon general session devoted to the discussion of specific readings."[41] A course on ancient Greek theater offered these details of planned activities: "We shall take these ancient plays and immerse ourselves in them. We shall read them aloud for each other, talk about them, and read them some more."[42] It went on to explain that students would also write as a group in structured sessions: "We shall have writing sessions in which each seminar in the whole group works on its adaptation of one of the dramatic myths."[43] A course on "Space, Time, and Form" scheduled weekly studio time for trouble-shooting specific projects. The problems addressed in the studio, it was explained, "will be carefully coordinated with the readings and other work of the program, so that all of us are working together on similar problems at similar times."[44] A course titled "Man and Art: the Renaissance and Now" made this simple promise: "Something will be 'doing' every week."[45]

Statements of this type served as placeholders for curriculum still under construction. They give a sense of the uncertainty that enveloped the nascent institution. They also reiterate the arguments made elsewhere in the catalog about the ways in which Evergreen is like other schools insofar as it entails academic commitments and obligations. If being educated is a matter of knowing how to read and write, they suggest, being college educated is a matter of learning to read and write in a particular way: to read thoroughly, to read aloud for others, to read some more, to write in a group. These statements describe a curriculum in which content acquisition is less important than the sustained and coordinated movement of academic study that the catalog refers to as devotion and immersion.

By describing conventional classroom practices in terms of movement, faculty transformed them from content vehicles into occasions. The course materials the catalog mentions might have been familiar, but the arrangement for studying them was not. It is the traditional function of the course catalog to inform students when and where a course will meet. When Evergreen published its first catalog, such administrative details had not yet been worked out. Nevertheless, the course descriptions refer to specific congregations planned for designated times. A student could always immerse herself in Greek tragedy on her own time. Evergreen's catalog issued an invitation to do so with others at a specific time and place: each week, in a group. How would the play sound then? How would it articulate with other activities? What would happen?

With its emphasis on occasions, Evergreen's catalog reflects a kairotic sense of time. The ancient Greeks had two words for time. *Chronos* refers to duration, age, frequency, and other measured forms. A progression of courses that lead through a course of study reflect this chronological sense of time. *Kairos* refers to the ordinality of events and the special place of the occasion that can only happen at a particular time.[46] It marks moments that call on us to address them and respond "at the proper time and in a fitting way."[47] Time and place converge in the notion of *kairos*; as Michel de Certeau describes it, *kairos* refers to the "right point in time."[48] In the more general sense of the word, kairotic moments might be distinguished by urgent matters, shaped by decorum as in the case of a seasonal ceremony, or simply appear opportune such as when a friend references a topic about which you have a good story thus generating an ideal time for you to tell it.[49]

Traditional models of education often present learning as a linear, chronological movement: instructors communicate established forms of knowledge and students advance through classes and grade levels. In some versions of informal education, such as the free school, education is less about progression than it is an attitude one adopts that enables education to happen any time. Evergreen's courses, in contrast, organized education around particular moments. This is in part why the faculty could not predict ahead of time what students would learn or do, or even what would happen. The catalog entry for the "Political Ecology" program, for instance, hedges its bets on whether the class will meet each week for a lecture or a film, "or perhaps to do both."[50] The course materials are given less weight than what will happen with them when read aloud or critiqued in a group or investigated in a laboratory. As it was structured at Evergreen, education was a series of encounters in which the act of encountering and how one negotiated that encounter, became more important than progression through materials or skill levels. The use of the present participle in the statement "something will be 'doing' every week" conveys this kairotic, event-oriented sense of educational time.

In focusing on occasions, Evergreen presented education as a matter of flexibility attuned to the moment. This approach to education is analogous to a sophistic notion of rhetoric and to some poststructuralist accounts of symbolic action. Among the points of overlap between rhetorical and poststructural theories is the idea that the force of speech "emerges in the encounter itself."[51] A speaker cannot know what to say until the moment arrives.[52] It is impossible to know what to say ahead of time because, from a rhetorical perspective, words do not carry an inherent power with them. Their power manifests in their deployment when they meet with objects, bodies, and phenomena. Meaning is mutable and language unstable. Language acquires its durability and becomes substantive through its usage while the world and the words we use to describe it become meaningful through speech acts.[53] Finding the right words is, then, a kairotic exercise: one must be open to possibilities in the moment to find the words appropriate to the situation.

The relationship that Evergreen faculty forged between "flexibility" and "place" resembles this situational perspective. As the curriculum developed, "place" became a verb and "flexibility" its quality. In Evergreen terms, knowledge was an event, not a destination. Becoming educated meant learning where and how to position one's self in a situation; how, for instance, to hear a play as it is read aloud by a peer. Learning was a matter of articulating seemingly disparate, unrelated topics and shuttling between different disciplinary approaches. Students would be responsible, the catalog explained, "for understanding and feeling the connections between ideas, techniques, and habits of thinking usually segregated in different departments."[54] The attention to calibrated movement is exemplified in the interdisciplinary design of each program, an approach premised on the understanding that the same object or topic might be studied from different angles. A classic text such as, for instance, *Moby Dick*, might have literary, historical, sociological, and scientific significance. Different situations obligate us to read artifacts in different ways, and knowing how to read becomes a matter of knowing what the situation calls for. A conventional classroom settles such matters by deciding the approach ahead of time; the free school often deferred to the interests of the individual student; an Evergreen course might launch a text along multiple currents at once, allowing for the possibility that it would carry the class in more than one direction or that the class might circulate through a text several times. Its place in the course, in other words, was not prescribed but neither was it without parameters. As it was explained in the catalog, the classes were "more than usually responsive to the internal requirements of the problems at hand."[55] Such an approach was in keeping with the belief that it was impossible to know how to proceed with a particular question, topic, or text until one was well into a program of study.

In his discussion of the sophists, Muckelbaur explains this seeming paradox in which one learns where to go by keeping on the move. He calls this "the repetition of differential movement."[56] Given the mutability of language, he explains, to keep moving is the only way to achieve clarity where clarity is "no longer simply a less opaque visual perspective at which one can arrive; it is not a location, but a style of movement. . . . One must continually go elsewhere."[57] Through repeat encounters made possible by such travel, we may come to know a subject or an object, not because we see it finally for what it actually is, but because we have encountered it in so many different ways. Going elsewhere might mean, as it often did in Evergreen's programs, circling back through the same object with a different set of questions, assignments, or participants.[58] The same encounter, repeated on a different register or at a different pace, could generate new insights.

The descriptive statements scattered throughout Evergreen's course catalog suggest the looping movement that Muckelbaur describes.[59] Some programs planned for it. A program titled "Human Development" scheduled a weekly lecture with the assumption that topics would emerge as the series progressed: "Students, staff, and community preceptors will meet as a group one evening a week to view a film or hear a lecture. Subsequent discussions will probably vary in setting and format as common interests, special interests, and patterns of friendship develop."[60] In the program "Causality, Freedom, and Chance," faculty seemed to have a similar expectation in mind when they planned a camping trip in the woods for the second quarter of the school year. As the catalog explained, "when most of the 'hard science' work is being done, another week in the woods is planned, to give people a chance to catch their breath and think about what has been happening."[61] These kinds of breaks and gaps in course schedules could seem indicative of a hesitancy to impose structure on students. It is possible to read these kinds of activities as invitations to "do your own thing." Yet the camping trip was not a break from class or from academic work; rather, it repositioned the hard work of science by moving it outdoors. Formal scientific study would continue during the camping trip, but it would take place under different circumstances, and if the choice of location seemed arbitrary (i.e., the connection between the woods and biological genetics less than self-evident), then what better activity for a class on chance? Indeed, chance was the element Cage introduced into his musical compositions in order to generate what he called happenings, or performances in which connections emerged due to simultaneity rather than causality.[62] In a similar spirit, the camping trip invited students to consider what might or what could emerge from the interplay between the woods, science, and caught breath.[63]

From Trajectories to Topoi

The question of what would happen in a course was two-part. There was the question of what would happen in the course and the question of what would happen as a result of the course. In the current language of assessment: what would be the learning outcomes? From the beginning, Evergreen employed common assessment measures to collect evidence of its impact such as, for instance, the number of its graduates with careers in regional business and government. It is difficult, however, to trace clear curricular trajectories through Evergreen's early documents. In Evergreen's catalog, the learning outcomes appear as mutable as the course content while in the program histories, faculty decline to make any claims about particular effects or outcomes. As one faculty member said at the end of the first year, "to wonder whether or not the Man and Art Program, or the first year of TESC was either a 'success or failure', is an exercise in absurdity."[64] The closest the catalog comes to something like an expected outcome is in the preface, which describes the kind of graduates that Evergreen hoped to produce: "flexible, widely informed persons who can adapt most readily and productively to the demands of our changing business world and who can become contributory participants in our nation's economic enterprise."[65] The faculty were wary of educational models that approached learning as progression through a linear body of knowledge. At the same time, they were wary of inadvertently replicating the traditional academic investment in specialization and of offering lessons so idiosyncratic that they were in effect nontransferable. [66] The question, then, of where to begin and end a course of study (with the particular or the general?) proved especially challenging.

Educational philosophy had taken up the question of transferability and the relationship between the particular and the general long before Evergreen faced it. Meiklejohn called it the "permanent problem of finding a 'content' basis for a scheme of liberal education."[67] Ideally, wrote Meiklejohn, a curriculum should have a sense of integrity; it should not be a collection of disparate materials and subjects, but should "hang together."[68] The educated mind, likewise, should be one in which its separate pieces "run into one another" or "have intellectual relations with one another."[69] The question educators must answer, argued Meiklejohn, was where to begin the development of such a mind: with the particular facts of a situation, or with general questions and ideas? Dewey spoke of the same problem in terms of continuity between experiences, and the interaction between situations. People carry experiences with them, he argued, from situation to situation, and those experiences, which in part come to define a situation, generate a sense of continuity (for better when it inclines toward the good or for the worse when it does not). [70] Dewey believed that educators should exercise judgment and actively arrange "worth-while" experiences for students. [71] However, education lay not in experience itself. For experience to be educative, he argued, it "must lead out into an expanding world of subject-matter."[72] And, he noted, it is a daunting task to attempt to design experiences that will incline students toward better habits of mind, however one defined those. Mucklebaur captures this pedagogical dilemma in a question long debated by teachers of rhetoric: "If singularity cannot be framed by a methodology and cannot even be finally reduced to intelligibility, what force can it have in a classroom?"[73] Put another way, can a general skill be acquired through encounters with singular situations?

When applied to Evergreen's bricolage programs, the question of how the particular mapped to the general underwent some revision. As many of the faculty remarked in their program histories, the programs unfolded about as well as could be expected, particularly in those first years while the college organized itself. That said, if students developed a flexible integrity with which to move in the world, it is not evidenced in the histories. That omission could be attributed to a lack of evidence, or it could mean that the faculty were interested in documenting something else, as seems to have been the case. Rather than show how a unique event such as a camping trip translated into a generally applicable skill like adaptability, the faculty instead used the program histories to document the emergent grounds for education that they were generating and to lend some definition to the college's unsettled place in the region, the state, and in higher education. The college's relative youth, its teaching and regional missions, the design of its extended interdisciplinary programs all gave reason to take a closer than usual look at the college's immediate surroundings and its institutional offerings. The program histories, a genre that appears to have been invented for the purpose of archiving Evergreen's unusual one-time courses, documented that self-reflexive work and captured some of the institutional rhythms that gradually wore grooves into the campus. What becomes apparent in the histories (that is not clear in the catalog) is that no program unfolded as an airy experiment. Something substantive was at stake in every course. What began in the catalog as a proposal for ways of arranging and viewing the world became consequential. One by one, the programs constituted the grounds for the inquiries and lessons Evergreen offered, both those underway and in the future. In documenting that process, the faculty were less concerned with showing results, or even mapping coherent trajectories, than they were in reflecting on the texture and conditions of the grounds they were inventing. Through that extended and collective process, they gradually and indirectly generated provisional answers to the question of where to begin a course of study.

The sense of place that Evergreen's program histories convey again finds a parallel in rhetorical studies. *Topoi*, the Greek word for places, is the spatial metaphor used in rhetoric to refer to "the places or seats of argument."[74] Ever since Aristotle attempted a taxonomy for the *topoi*, the concept has generated a debate (analogous to the general/particular question) about how best to distinguish the topics appropriate only to specific situations, and those which are widely applicable, or commonplace.[75] Carolyn Miller suggests that Aristotle may have conceptualized the topics as having both specific and common elements, or of arguments being of both an exclusive and a shared place.[76] This idea of a dynamic between the specific and the common lends itself to more generative notions of rhetoric and to what Barbara A. Biesecker calls the second dimension of the rhetorical situation.[77] As Meiklejohn noted, if not even "general" and "specific" are stable designations, the question of where a topic begins and ends is enormous. To this Biesecker adds that designating the grounds or place of rhetorical address is itself a rhetorical act. If "rhetorical" refers to the means by which we express an idea, a second dimension of the rhetorical situation is "the initial formative intervention that, in centering a differential situation, makes possible the production of meaning."[78] Before we can identify the words appropriate to a situation, we must first formulate the situation itself and we do so from some place, "a located perspective from which one searches."[79] Working with a generative notion of rhetoric, Richard McKeon extends that argument to the process of inquiry, explaining that "we do not find subject-matters ready made nor do we encounter problems distributed precisely in fields. We make subject-matters to fit the examination."[80] Making those determinations, Biesecker argues, is as much a rhetorical act as any response we might generate to the situation, which is why, she suggests, when we think of rhetoric as producing its own grounds of possibility, it makes more sense to think of it "as governed by a logic of articulation rather than influence."[81] Rhetorical action is as much a matter of constituting the grounds for our position as it is persuading others to adopt that position. The two actions may not even be distinct.

These accounts of *topoi* and of the rhetorical situation offer one way of valuing the institution building documented in Evergreen's program histories. If read in our contemporary terms of assessment, the program histories simply confirm a number of academic commonplaces: learning processes are disjointed (no matter how well structured); whether a class "gels" or not is always to some degree a matter of luck; human education is a time and resource-intensive affair. If instead we apply a situated sense of place to the program histories, they show us the efforts of the faculty to articulate unique grounds for education. That is to say, the histories show how, beyond simply accessing the living laboratories surrounding the campus or merging disciplinary perspectives with world affairs, the college itself became education. From this perspective, the purpose of the program histories was to document and reflect on those processes.

A passage from the history of "Man and Art," a program led by José Arguelles, Cruz Esquivel, and Donald Chan, illustrates how as early as 1971, the material grounds of the college itself became both the subject and source of education. With all of the campus buildings still under construction, Evergreen held its first year of classes in borrowed buildings and other temporary spaces. Arguelles, Esquivel, and Chan describe how the first quarter unfolded in their borrowed space and how the space itself shaped the curriculum of their program:

> Man and Art opened in trauma headquarters (alias civil defense bldg . . ., on Martin Way, eastside); spent October schizophrenically between Seattle and limbo; began adjusting to concrete walls, institutional carpeting and plastic mass-produced chairs in modular windowless seminar rooms; found out it had no facilities for music, languages or practice of arts; found out coping with the situation was more important than finding out about the Medici; made batiks in an abandoned dance hall seventeen miles away; tried to stay calm but sometimes became hysterical; managed to give Evergreen its first concert and happening despite everything.[82]

Arguelles, Esquivel, and Chan's sensitivity to circumstance was not unique. Other faculty likewise used the program histories to reflect on and revise the conditions of education they were producing. Such was the case for the history of a 1973–1974 program called "Life on Earth" led by faculty members Linda Kahan, Chester Royse, and Peter Taylor. Their history begins with an account of "significant activities," that include several multi-day field trips to the OMSI field station at Camp Hancock and to San Juan Island. On those trips, students "collected fossils, toured several geographical provinces of Washington and observed a number of large scale geological phenomena, collected a variety of living invertebrates from a number of habitats, got an introduction to laboratory observations of living animals and began to keep their field notebooks."[83] This inventory suggests that students were moving through a recognized course of scientific education. Nevertheless, the faculty encountered problems with running "parallel" and "unrelated" lessons in geography, zoology, and oceanography.[84] Such a design fragmented student attention and prevented faculty from pooling their teaching efforts. To remedy the problem, faculty proposed even greater specificity and specialization in future programs:

> It is most important that the theme be given utmost prominence in the design and day-to-day activities of the program . . . the particular disciplines of the faculty must be subordinated to the theme rather than the opposite condition. . . . The lectures, seminars, films, reading, etc. should all relate to the particular subject. . . . For example, one period could concentrate on coral reefs. With the present faculty . . . a coordinated mixture . . . could be offered with contributions about coral animals and other reef organisms from Linda, about the formation and geological history of coral reefs by Chet and about environmental factors and the interrelationships of organisms by Pete. [85]

Here is an instance of Evergreen's endlessly flexible structure gaining coherence in the form of a conceptual place: the meeting point between the specifics of the northwest landscape, such as "rocky intertidal shores [and] submarine continental shelves," and the interdisciplinary expertise of the faculty. Kahan, Royse, and Taylor cautioned against the "temptation to offer comprehensive coverage of conventional subjects."[86] The goal was not to move students through a set course of materials but to actualize a unique set of educational circumstances.

To that end, Kahan, Royse, and Taylor also evaluated the organization of the field trips, noting that the class had used twelve private cars to transport sixty people. "To take a group of 100," they remarked, "would require 20 cars," an arrangement that would prove "expensive, time consuming, and very dangerous."[87] More than mere logistics, they saw in it an aspect of educational equity: "field trips are essential components of all curricula in earth and life sciences . . . and to the extent that students have to foot the bills for transportation as they have in this program, science programs will discriminate against the financially pressed student."[88] What they initially present as a logistical problem becomes part of their reflection on the kind of learning conditions they wish to cultivate, in this case, more equitable ones.

Teaching to the Situation

The catalog description and the history of a program titled "Contemporary American Minorities," which ran during the 1971–1972 school year, offers another example of how faculty were thinking about the learning conditions they wished to cultivate even while designing programs that would "self-destruct" at the end of the school year. It offers a stark example of how one-off programs made lasting contributions to the college and laid groundwork for future classes and inquires. In hindsight, the program appears to be a precursor to what are now more stable Evergreen offerings, including the Native American and World Indigenous Peoples Studies program, the Tacoma campus, which serves primarily minority students, and the college's extension programs at several Native American reservations. To read "Contemporary American Minorities" as an origin story, however, is to credit its faculty with more foresight than is possible and to erase the risk, experimentation, and uncertainty that went into the six-page course description that ran in the 1971 catalog.

Evergreen's interdisciplinary curriculum and its unconventional treatment of the credit hour troubled the prepositional phrases commonly used in higher education. Without terms like "discipline," "department," and "major" with which to organize topics into course sequences that in turn fulfilled degree requirements, the relationship between subjects could be endlessly reconfigured and might be propelled as much by the changing currents of social movements as by the predictable winds of tradition. At a traditional school, for instance, Evergreen's program "The Play's the Thing: Then and Now," might have been a class *on* theater that begins *with* Greek plays. Evergreen's catalog reconfigured that conventional arrangement so that "The Play's the Thing" was a program *about* law, order, freedom, and responsibility *in* the present day.[89]

The flexible form of Evergreen's programs allowed not only for adjustments to traditional approaches but also accommodated inchoate articulations between topics that might be worked out more fully as the class unfolded. This aspect of Evergreen's curriculum proved valuable to emergent and under-studied subjects and for topics ignored elsewhere in higher education. To suggest a connection between Greek tragedy and themes like law, order, and freedom was not without precedent, but a program on law, order, freedom, and the political economy of racial difference faced questions about whether such a subject even existed.[90] The six-page catalog description for "Contemporary American Minorities" argued that it did despite the unwillingness of white Americans to acknowledge it:

> The "melting pot" image of American society only partly describes life in the United States. Those not successfully "melted" into the "pot" have been Non-

whites. The White population, trapped in the fantasy of "one nation, indivisible" has been unwilling and unable to accept the fact of cultural difference.[91]

To run a program that acknowledged cultural difference without replicating racist logics, the program faulty organized racial and ethnic identity by the metonymic colors black, brown, red, and white and designed syllabi for different ethnic groups. "There will be," the faculty explained, "Black seminars, Red seminars, Brown seminars, a White seminar, and a mixed seminar" and "each ethnic seminar will have its own reading list, designed to stress careful study of the central problems in each subculture."[92] This was the faculty's answer to the question of where a student ought to begin not only the study of cultural difference but also "specialized work in history, sociology, law, anthropology, teaching, counseling, social work, literature, government, and community planning."[93] As was true of all the programs Evergreen hosted, it was a provisional answer to a reoccurring question.

The catalog description for "Contemporary American Minorities" gives the impression that the program planned to track students by racial and ethnic identity. Such an approach no doubt raised some questions about whether race and ethnicity should determine educational experience. The program history submitted by faculty members Medardo Delgado, Rudolph Martin, and Darrell Phare suggests the design was not intended to track students, but to give them a sense of 'territory'."[94] Their objective was to enable students of color to position themselves on the campus rather than have a place designated for them. It was an approach that acknowledged the ways in which education was always already circumscribed by broader social structures. If what a student studied, and how, when, and with whom they studied it mattered, then where a student positioned herself in the institution was as important as access to the institution.

As was evident in many of the program histories, the faculty of "Contemporary American Minorities" did not agree on how the program had fared. They echoed some of the frustrations voiced in other histories: Students were unprepared. Their "analytical reading, critical thinking, significant research and serious study were spotty."[95] Students who left the program "complained about too little or too much structure"; seminar discussions often wound around in circles; everyone struggled with Evergreen's experimental design.[96] Even so, the faculty agreed that the program proved worthwhile: "most students and the faculty learned a lot and profited from the experience [in] some ways that defy measurement, though much of what they learned was not traditional [in] academic terms."[97]

Despite their frustrations, Delgado, Martin, and Phare provide an impressive inventory of tangible accomplishments that included internship hours completed, productions made, and associations established.[98] Their accomplishments included "community service at the Chehalis Indian reservation and at Frank's Landing, in Tacoma's black community, in Chicano-oriented political action, and in Olympia and Centralia public schools."[99] Students in the program also organized three campus associations for students of color: Ujamaa Society, MECHA, and NASA. The associations, the faculty explained, "transcend the traditional students organizations in that they work in the areas of curriculum, faculty and student recruitment, community relations and in all areas of TESC life relating to non-white people."[100] That work, they went on to explain, realized one of the goals for the program: "to give non-white students at Evergreen a viable physical and emotional foundation from which to pursue their present and future college training."[101] The program inspired a call issued in April 1972 to address "the absence of minority concerns in the remainder of TESC's academic programs" and "for the complete, systematic inclusion of the minority experience in all programs where relevant."[102] As the faculty explained, whatever ground the program had established was not intended to be permanent. It was "a band-aid on a large wound."[103] It was nevertheless ground for further action.

It Was Education While It Was Happening

A program's yield did not always take the form of community projects or curricular revisions as it did in the case of "Contemporary American Minorities." Where a program did not unfold as the faculty had hoped, its contributions to Evergreen's curriculum might come in the form of less tangible, inconclusive observations on how to organize studies in the future. Such was the case with "Towards Humane Technospheres" a program that ran in the 1974–1975 school year. "Technospheres" was taught by Richard Alexander, Robert Knapp, and Bob Filmer. Alexander, who wrote the bulk of the program history, explains that "Technospheres" began as a "long-standing desire on the part of Rob Knapp."[104] Knapp himself explains that he had "hoped for a joint effort of unraveling the strands of human intention and natural law that give our technological society its particular character."[105] The faculty designed workshops in technical skills and organized case studies in four industries—wood, transportation, energy, and computers, "all clearly relevant to the Pacific Northwest."[106] They reserved space in the curriculum for philosophical reflection on the meaning of "humane" and its future prospects. A list of student final projects include a study of Olympia's food markets, construction of a twelve-foot windcharger, redesign of a dorm room to better accommodate a person in a wheelchair, and a study of occupant involvement in public housing.

Alexander stops short of speculating on what students or even faculty took away from the program and bases his evaluation instead on the internal texture of the course itself. Of the final spring quarter, Alexander writes: "Since there seems to be nothing here that really could be recommended to the planners of future programs, I think I will drop the topic, concluding simply with the comment that this period felt really quite comfortable and natural while it was happening, and was by no means a loss of any sort."[107] His observations are in keeping with the attention given in other histories to the institutional conditions of education. On this point, Alexander expresses confidence in the value of the educational time and place that "Technospheres" produced. While it may seem that Alexander's evaluation of "Technospheres" is expressed as a negative (i.e., nothing to recommend) and thus makes no long-term contribution to the campus, his narrative models the usefulness to higher education of a situational sensibility. In noting Knapp's long-standing desire, a last-minute change in faculty, and a number of other logistical adaptations made as the course progressed, the program history expresses appreciation for the convergence of circumstance and exhibits an eye for possibility. Alexander takes the time, for instance, to mention the influence one student made on the course.

> The one student who made serious contributions [during the initial planning] was Sarah Gunning, who argued for heavy inclusion of women's materials. . . . But Ms. Gunning did not at last join the program, and her major contribution therefore was to inspire Knapp to explore the relevant literature on women and industry, and thereby to discover Janeway's *Man's World, Woman's Place*.[108]

His point with this story seems to be that while the meandering and resource-intensive process of organizing a course could disappoint in the scale of its impact, it is nevertheless worthwhile insofar as it produces conditions that would not have existed otherwise and by any other means. With that insight, Alexander's evaluation goes beyond an exercise in documenting the impact of a single class. It offers an altogether different way of thinking about the value of the academic project and the purpose to education of institutional structure.

To cultivate at other colleges and universities the situational sensibility that Alexander and his colleagues exhibit does not require an adoption of the Evergreen model. Other schools may, however, benefit from the appreciation for detail and circumstance modeled in Evergreen's course descriptions and program histories. If other schools appear to be more alike one another than Evergreen is different, that may be only because they have less incentive to document their institutional processes as Evergreen has done. Evergreen's most significant contribution to higher education may be the alternative narrative of academic life that it provides. In a similar vein, the following chapter compiles interviews with faculty from Evergreen and CSUMB on how and why they came to teach at those campuses, and the professional obligations and personal interests that have shaped their work. Those personal narratives depart from the standard professional academic script and show another layer of the institutional circumstance that shapes the academic project.

NOTES

1. Statement by Dr. Garrett Heyns, Olympia; President of Southwestern Washington State College Committee, at joint public hearing of Senate and House Committees on Higher Education, in House Chamber, 7:30 p.m., February 15, 1967 (p. 4).

2. Ibid.

3. "The Evergreen State College at a Glance," (Olympia, WA: 1970), 1. Malcolm Stilson Archives and Special Collections, The Evergreen State College, Olympia, WA. This same language appears in the inaugural course catalog in a section that explains how the campus design "supports Evergreen's philosophy that learning extends beyond the classroom, providing students a large living outdoor laboratory for environmental, marine, and other scientific study." "The Evergreen State College 1971–72 Bulletin," (Olympia, WA), 156. Malcolm Stilson Archives and Special Collections, The Evergreen State College, Olympia, WA.

4. William Henry Stevens III, "The Philosophical and Political Origins of the Evergreen State College" (PhD diss., University of Washington, 1983), 156–57. Malcolm Stilson Archives and Special Collections, The Evergreen State College, Olympia, WA. When approval for a new state college finally came in 1964, the Washington State Council of Presidents looked to a 1960 citizen's committee report on higher education for guidance. The report argued the need to recognize different talents and realize individual potential.

5. Senator Gordon Sandison paraphrased in the Minutes of the Board of Trustees New Four Year College, Office of the Governor (Olympia, Washington, August 30, 1967), 3. Malcolm Stilson Archives and Special Collections, The Evergreen State College, Olympia, WA.

6. Stevens III, "Philosophical and Political Origins."

7. Aaron J. Brumbaugh, "Establishing New Senior Colleges," Southern Regional Education Board Monograph, no. 12 (1966): 4. Brumbaugh cheered the diversity of the U.S. system of higher education. "Only a monolithic society," he wrote, "can justify a monolithic system of higher education." Ibid., 2.

8. Ibid., 42.

9. Ibid., 44–45.

10. "The Evergreen State College 1971–72 Bulletin," (Olympia, WA), 12. Malcolm Stilson Archives and Special Collections, The Evergreen State College, Olympia, WA. A 1970 progress report described the curriculum as "designed to help young people adapt to the changing needs of business, industry and society" and oriented toward "problem solving" and "continuing learning." "The Evergreen State College: Facts, Figures, and Forecasts for the Future" (September 1970): 2.

11. Richard M. Jones, *Experiment at Evergreen* (Cambridge, MA: Schenkman Books, 1981). Richard M. Jones documents another layer of the Evergreen model in his reflections on the student evaluation process. In *Experiment at Evergreen*, he includes the full text of evaluations he wrote for several Evergreen students along with personal correspondence between him and the students. While his objective differs from mine in that he argues the value of a particular pedagogical philosophy and practice, his approach to student evaluations reflects the situational sensibility illustrated in the program histories.

12. Ron Miller, *Free Schools, Free People: Education and Democracy after the 1960s* (Albany: State University of New York Press, 2002), 2–3.

13. Allen Graubard, *Free the Children: Radical Reform and the Free School Movement* (New York: Vintage Books, 1972), 124; The Elizabeth Cleaners Street School, *Starting Your Own High School* (New York: Random House, 1972). The Santa Barbara Community School, for instance, operated out of a park and then parents' homes. The Elizabeth Cleaners Street School opened in Fall 1970 in Manhattan's Upper West Side. Unable to afford rent, parents and students researched squatting and then occupied a building one Saturday afternoon.

14. Ivan Illich, *Deschooling Society* (New York: Harper & Row, 1970), 25. In his study of the free school movement, Graubard explains the distinction educators made between "noncoercion" or "self-motivation" and the organization of a curriculum from "the conceptions the students have of their own interests, concerns, ideals, values, and future expectations" (Graubard, *Free the Children*, 92–93).

15. Graubard, *Free the Children*. Graubard describes free school curricula that include a number of topics made possible by community contacts who were able to teach, including Chicano history, auto maintenance, German drama, and volleyball.

16. Mervyn L. Cadwallader who later joined Evergreen's founding faculty organized San Jose State's General Program Experiment between 1965 and 1969.

17. Mervyn L. Cadwallader, "Experiment at San Jose," A Paper Presented to the Conference on Alternative Higher Education," (The Evergreen State College, Olympia, WA, 1981): 1–43. As Cadwallader explains in his history of the program at San Jose State College, he attributed student disillusionment to "dull textbooks," "dull lectures," and "machine-graded objective examinations" (8).

18. "Dreams: From the Franconia College Catalog, 1964," in *Five Experimental Colleges: Bensalem, Antioch-Putney, Franconia, Old Westbury, Fairhaven*, ed. Gary B. MacDonald (New York: Harper & Row, 1973), 106.

19. Ibid., 110.

20. Ibid.,111.

21. Jonathan Kozol, *Free Schools* (New York: Bantam Books, 1972); Ann Swidler, *Organization without Authority: Dilemmas of Social Control in Free Schools* (Cambridge, MA: Harvard University Press, 1979).

22. Eva Díaz, *The Experimenters: Chance and Design at Black Mountain College* (Chicago: University of Chicago Press, 2015), 104; Díaz attributes much of this philosophy to Josef Albers, an influential member of the Black Mountain faculty. Albers believed, Díaz argues, that with "all the attention given to the [artistic] artifacts of the past, the *process* of creation had become neglected." Díaz, 47.

23. Charles J. McCann, 3. Malcolm Stilson Archives and Special Collections, The Evergreen State College, Olympia, WA:http://archives.evergreen.edu/1971/1971-01/mccann_institutionalgoals.pdf

24. Charles J. McCann, 5. Malcolm Stilson Archives and Special Collections, The Evergreen State College, Olympia, WA: http://www.evergreen.edu/facultydevelopment/docs/ABriefHistory1967-73Kormondy.pdf

25. John Dewey, *Experience and Education* (Detroit, MI: Free Press, 1938), 23.

26. Charles J. McCann, "Institutional Goals and Statement of Purpose," 2. Malcolm Stilson Archives and Special Collections, The Evergreen State College, Olympia, WA: http://archives.evergreen.edu/1971/1971-01/mccann_institutionalgoals.pdf

27. Joseph Shoben, "Some thoughts, mostly random, about both buildings and academic program," Memorandum dated October 13, 1969 addressed to President McCann. Malcolm Stilson Archives and Special Collections, The Evergreen State College, Olympia, WA. In another memo, Shoben proposes a possible curricular organization (four broad interdisciplinary divisions lead by deans) and argues that the re-design will need to extend to faculty and administrators themselves: "In creating the broadest possible bounds within which students can exercise individual initiative and personal responsibility in defining the parameters of their education, Evergreen's professors and administrative officers must simultaneously structure themselves in the light of that student-oriented objective" (4). Joseph Shoben, "Another pass at academic organization and the curriculum at TESC," Memorandum dated November 10, 1969 addressed to President Charles McCann and Vice Presidents David Barry and Dean Clabaugh. Malcolm Stilson Archives and Special Collections, The Evergreen State College, Olympia, WA.

28. The Evergreen State College Planning Conference, February 8–9, 1970, Tape I. 1, Side A. (1:11:28). Malcolm Stilson Archives and Special Collections, The Evergreen State College, Olympia, WA.

29. Julian Sefton-Green, "Cultural Studies and Education: Reflecting on Differences, Impacts, Effects and Change," *Cultural Studies* 25, no. 1 (2011): 67. The education philosophy

that conflates learning with life itself has a long history, but it became especially pronounced in the 1960s and 70s during which time an estimated four hundred "free schools" opened (and closed) along side hundreds of other short-lived alternative educational projects. In 1966, for instance, Berkeley students "began organizing spontaneous classes to replace those they were boycotting" and in the spring of that year, they organized the Free University of Berkeley. Miller, *Free Schools*, 3.

30. David Marr and S.R. "Rudy" Martin, "M 'n M Manifesto: My Snowman's Burning Down" (March 9, 1972): 2. Malcolm Stilson Archives and Special Collections, The Evergreen State College, Olympia, WA.

31. "The Evergreen State College, 1971–1972 Bulletin" (Olympia, WA), 2. Malcolm Stilson Archives and Special Collections, The Evergreen State College, Olympia, WA.

32. Ibid., 3.

33. Ibid., 89.

34. Ibid., 89–90.

35. Not even the titles of the histories are consistent. One group referred to it as a self-evaluation, another called it "Evergreen's First Year Collective History," and another group called it an autobiography.

36. Byron L. Youtz, "The Evergreen State College: An Experiment Maturing," (1981), 6. Malcolm Stilson Archives and Special Collections, The Evergreen State College, Olympia, WA.

37. "1971–1972 Bulletin," 21.

38. "The Evergreen State College 1971–72 Bulletin" (Olympia, WA), 51.

39. Ibid., 55.

40. Ibid.

41. Ibid., 75.

42. Ibid., 53.

43. Ibid., 54.

44. Ibid., 66.

45. Ibid., 81.

46. John E. Smith, "Time, Times, and the 'Right Time': 'Chronos' and 'Kairos,'" *The Monist* 53, no. 1 (January 1969): 1–13.

47. John Muckelbauer, *The Future of Invention: Rhetoric, Postmodernism, and the Problem of Change* (Albany: State University of New York Press, 2008), 114.

48. Michel De Certeau, *The Practice of Everyday Life* (Trans.) Steven Rendall (Berkeley: University of California Press, 1984), 82. Certeau mentions *kairos* in his discussion of *mêtis*, a form of situational knowledge often translated as cunning. The relationship between *kairos*, *mêtis*, and the situation, he explains, is an economical one: "The occasion is encyclopedic because of *mêtis*'s ability to use through it its treasure of past experiences and to inventory multiple possibilities in it: it contains all this knowledge within the smallest volume. It concentrates the most knowledge in the least time."

49. Dale L. Stephens, "*Kairos* and the Rhetoric of Belief," *Quarterly Journal of Speech* 78 (1992): 317–32. *Kairos* had varied and textured meanings. Dale L. Stephens identifies three meanings of *kairos* used by the sophist Gorgias in his *Encomium of Helen*: "a poetic timing that produces connections and thus a special logos, a point of indecision encountered when competing opinions are presented, and a sort of irrational power that makes decision possible" (319).

50. "The Evergreen State College, 1971–1972 Bulletin," (Olympia, WA), 55.

51. Debra Hawhee, "Kairotic Encounters" in *Perspectives on Rhetorical Invention*, ed. Janet M. Atwill and Janice M. Lauer (Knoxville: The University of Tennessee Press, 2002), 31.

52. Debra Hawhee, *Bodily Arts: Rhetoric and Athletics in Ancient Greece* (Austin: University of Texas Press, 2004), 44–64. For an extended discussion of this idea in Ancient Greece, see Hawhee's study of sophistic *mêtis* or the art of cunning and timely craftiness often represented in art with images of octopuses and wrestlers.

53. Sharon Crowley, "Of Gorgias and Grammatology," *College Composition and Communication* 30 (1979): 279–283; Richard Lanham, "The Rhetorical Paideia: The Curriculum as a Work of Art." *College English* 48, no. 2 (1986): 132–41. For a map of the resonances between sophistic rhetoric and poststructuralism see Sharon Crowley and Richard Lanham. Evergreen

faculty may or may not have been directly influenced by either the sophists or poststructuralism. I am borrowing that language to show the differences between traditional and free school approaches.

54. "1971–1972 Bulletin," 20.

55. Ibid., 21.

56. Muckelbaur, *Future of Invention,* 93.

57. Ibid.

58. Some critics find Evergreen less rigorous than other colleges because classes may have only a few assigned readings. That conclusion makes sense from a model of education in which course materials deliver information rather than serving as objects of study that can be engaged and discussed again and again.

59. Muckelbaur, *Future of Invention,* 43. Muckelbaur elsewhere describes this movement as "a relay on an intensive, inventional circuit."

60. "1971–1972 Bulletin," 46.

61. Ibid., 34.

62. Díaz, *The Experimenters.* Cage composed and performed his first happening, *Theater Piece No. 1,* in collaboration with other faculty at Black Mountain College in 1952.

63. Mario Untersteiner, *The Sophists,* trans. Kathleen Freeman (Oxford: Blackwell, 1954), 111. Mario Untersteiner ascribes to the sophists a poetic sense of *kairos* that referred to the possibility of moments—instances like the trip to the woods "in which the intimate connection between things is realized."

64. "Man and Art" program history, p. 7.

65. "1971–1972 Bulletin," 14.

66. The Evergreen State College Planning Conference, February 8–9, 1970, Tape I. 1, Side A. Malcolm Stilson Archives and Special Collections, The Evergreen State College, Olympia, WA. The matter of over specialization was raised several times at the 1970 Planning Conference.

67. Alexander Meiklejohn, *The Experimental College* (Madison: University of Wisconsin Press, 1932), 66.

68. Ibid., 45.

69. Ibid., 46.

70. Dewey, *Experience and Education,* 13. The "principle of continuity of experience," Dewey explained, "means that every experience both takes up something from those which have gone before and modifies in some way the quality of those which come after."

71. Ibid., 18.

72. Ibid., 39.

73. Muckelbaur, *Future of Invention,* 120.

74. Richard McKeon, *Rhetoric: Essays in Invention and Discovery* (Woodbridge, CT: Ox Bow Press, 1987), 14.

75. Carolyn R. Miller, "Aristotle's 'Special Topics' in Rhetorical Practice and Pedagogy," *Rhetoric Society Quarterly* 17 (Winter 1987): 61–70.

76. Carolyn R. Miller, "The Aristotelian Topos: Hunting for Novelty," in *Rereading Aristotle's Rhetoric,* eds. Alan G. Gross and Arthur E. Walzer (Carbondale: Southern Illinois University Press, 2000): 135.

77. Barbara A. Biesecker, "Rethinking the Rhetorical Situation from within the Thematic of *Différance,*" *Philosophy and Rhetoric* 22 (1989): 110–30.

78. Biesecker, "Rethinking the Rhetorical," 112.

79. Miller, Aristotelian Topos, 141.

80. McKeon, *Rhetoric,* 17.

81. Biesecker, "Rethinking the Rhetorical," 112.

82. "Man and Art," 6.

83. Linda Kahan, Chester Royse, and Peter Taylor, "Life on Earth Program History, 1973." Malcolm Stilson Archives and Special Collections, The Evergreen State College, Olympia, WA.

84. "Life on Earth," 5.

85. Ibid., 6.

86. Ibid.

87. Ibid., 3.

88. Ibid.

89. The catalog description suggests all three possibilities (see pp. 53–54).

90. The catalog description includes all of these terms except for "order" and "responsibility," though it does include the phrase "to assume active, important roles" and the word "conformed" (36, 37).

91. "1971–1972 Bulletin," 37.

92. Ibid., 39.

93. Ibid., 41.

94. Delgago Medardo, Rudolph Martin, and Darrell Phare. "Contemporary American Minorities Program History—Self Evaluation, Faculty Edition," 1972. Malcolm Stilson Archives and Special Collections, The Evergreen State College, Olympia, WA.

95. Ibid., 3.

96. "Contemporary American Minorities Program History," 3.

97. Ibid., 5.

98. The difference between "accomplishments" and "accumulations of time" was noted at the 1970 planning meeting and may have been a notion that circulated the campus (23:17).

99. "Contemporary American Minorities Program History," 3.

100. Ibid.

101. Ibid., 1.

102. "Future Academic plans for minority people at TESC," Letter dated April 19, 1972. Malcolm Stilson Archives and Special Collections, The Evergreen State College, Olympia, WA.

103. Ibid.

104. Richard Alexander with Robert Knapp, and Bob Filmer, "Program History: Toward Humane Technospheres," 1974–75. Malcolm Stilson Archives and Special Collections, The Evergreen State College, Olympia, WA.

105. Ibid., 24.

106. Ibid., 7.

107. Ibid., 22.

108. Ibid., 4.

Chapter Two

The Strangely Appropriate
Texture of Academic Life

In its twenty-fifth year, CSUMB retained the feel of its predecessor, Fort Ord. Coastal succulents and pine trees flattened by the wind grew in the sandy tracts of land between single story cement buildings. The campus street names—General Jim Moore Boulevard and Colonel Durham Street—recalled former occupants. Barracks and training facilities were now classrooms, dorms, and offices, some of them still furnished with metal chairs and desks inherited from the army. A half-century-old autoclave sat in the hallway of what was once the Fort's dental building and is now home to the Water Shed Institute. In his history of the campus, CSUMB professor Gerald Shenk relays an anecdote that marvels at other unexpected connections between the former and current campuses.

> [A colleague] was scavenging for bits and pieces of Army history in the abandoned buildings on this former Army post. He came across the curriculum manual for a leadership training program. . . . At the top of the first page was a definition of teaching: "Teaching is the creation of conditions under which learning may occur."[1]

Shenk found it "strangely appropriate," he goes on to say, that the university which had replaced the Fort "on this spot of land overlooking Monterey Bay" had begun "its life with a similar approach to education."[2] He is referring in this instance to the coherence between the army's teaching philosophy and the critical pedagogy that shaped the university. Where some might attribute that coherence to the nature of teaching, Shenk's description of it as both appropriate *and* strange suggests an inventive element at work. His deliberate

45

pairing exemplifies the careful attention that CSUMB faculty have paid to the young university's conditions for learning.

Shenk's anecdote honors the inventive practices that forge educational circumstance. It is easier to see those practices at an unusual, makeshift campus like CSUMB than at more established schools. It is harder to see the impermanent and circumstantial aspects of education in its more routinized forms. Traditional campuses denote permanence and stability. They appear secure against provincialism and unburdened by the present moment. Shared policies and procedures, such as the articulation agreements that enable credit transfers or the boilerplate language that appears in syllabi, ensure consistency and legitimacy. The myth of the ivory tower is that any given college campus could reside anywhere, unchanged. The myth does not hold at CSUMB where no one could fail to notice its unfinished elements or miss the peculiar feel of a campus built from a former army base. Where ivy-covered brick campuses look timeless, it looks fused to its location, as if it could only be as it is, where it is.

CSUMB is today home to a military archive. The street names and the murals with army chevrons are now a recognized part of the learning conditions on that coastal campus, but even that outcome was not always certain. Academic codes of professionalism affirm the value of preservation efforts, but they do not ensure which histories will be archived. One former president of CSUMB sought to remove all traces of the military until her plan proved unpopular with the campus and local residents. Critics of her plan appealed to the university's specific commitments to boundary-crossing and community collaboration in an effort to preserve the remaining vestiges of military life. The critics won. Then it took curious faculty sifting through abandoned filing cabinets and other military flotsam to fold that history into the emergent university.[3]

CSUMB's campus is unusual in some respects and representative in others. Academic institutions are bound by tradition, policy, and professional convention, but they are not static. Even established colleges and universities continuously reconstitute the grounds of education by renaming buildings, revising their histories, and reorganizing their curricula.[4] While those practices follow familiar rhythms, they always generate distinctive patterns. That pliable work often takes place in the interstices, or what Dwight Conquergood describes as the "*in between* structures."[5] Some of it takes recognizable and expected institutional forms and some of it results in what Jean and John Comaroff describe as "intimate, if invisible, connections across dimensions and scales."[6]

Among the contributions CSUMB and Evergreen have made to higher education is the heightened visibility of their institutional organization. Their visibility stems from their alternative curricula, which in turn have enabled each campus to explore the iterative, situated, and generative dimensions of academic work. Some of those efforts have generated distinctive and enduring materials, such as CSUMB's military archive. Much of it flashes for a moment and disappears, but even those fleeting moments have a heightened quality. While giving me a campus tour, Shenk shared a story about a class that ran in CSUMB's early years. It met in the evenings in an un-renovated building with spotty electricity. When the lamps overhead occasionally went out, everyone pulled their desks closer to the windows, and closer to each other, to catch the failing light. Peter Simonson speaks about such situations "with bodies gathered together in a particular room," harboring possibilities and furnishing invention.[7] In this case, the classroom conditions illuminated questions that may never have surfaced in a fully wired classroom, such as what it means to persevere through structural inequity to pursue an education.

This chapter relays five other stories about inventive work at CSUMB and at Evergreen. The stories come from members of the faculty and each one tells of iterative projects that draw on the skills and personal know-how born of professional life. In each case, faculty members made decisions from the options at hand and then navigated the possibilities that opened and closed as a result. Just as the alternative curricula at these schools helps to make visible the work that goes into arranging and situating education, it likewise makes the inventiveness of the faculty's work easier to see. Their work, moreover, exemplifies a situational sensibility. Each one approaches academia's fragmented, inconsistent, and incommensurable infrastructure as an asset rather than a shortcoming. Each navigates unusual campus conditions with unconventional decisions that result in strangely appropriate contributions.

The ancient Greeks had two terms for the kind of knowledge that situational work entails and they applied those terms to crafts as varied as seafaring, politics and teaching.[8] *Techne* is useful for maneuvering in and around constraints. What most distinguishes *techne*'s domain, argues Atwill, is its concern with "what is possible" as opposed to what is necessary or determined.[9] Jay Dolmage describes *techne*'s companion *mêtis* in similar terms. *Mêtis* interacts with and circumscribes "the world of chance and opportunity."[10] Hawhee argues that a corporeal dimension distinguishes *techne* and *mêtis* from other types of knowledge, such as *episteme*.[11] *Mêtis* in particular reflects the timeliness of embodied know-how exemplified by athletic reflexes.[12] It is suited to "complex and nonrepeatable" environments and "shifting or ambiguous situations."[13] Eric Charles White describes *mêtis* as the "speculatively mobile form of interpretation" that a kairotic world requires and Michelle Ballif describes it as the "ways and means to negotiate the flux."[14] The following five stories model this type of movement across a changing environment. The work is oriented toward the possible. It is responsive to chance. It negotiates complex terrain with timely, unpredictable turns. Col-

lectively, these stories offer an interpretive heuristic that cues us to look for a
certain kind of situated, opportune, speculative dimension to academic work
that conventional accounts rarely capture. The stories lend visibility to similar work underway at other campuses by showing us what to look for and
how to see it.

Inventing the Perfect Fit

The story of how Shenk came to CSUMB illustrates the extent to which
personal details can shape educational practices. The connection is especially
pronounced in his case because his story parallels the history of the campus.
Shenk began teaching at CSUMB in 1996 in the university's second year, but
his faculty appointment was not the first job that brought Shenk to that
campus. Before pursuing an academic career and while living in San Francisco in the 1970s, Shenk worked with an organization that provided legal
counsel to enlisted men. He occasionally accompanied soldiers who had
gone AWOL to Fort Ord to be discharged. His work with a Quaker organization again brought him to Fort Ord to visit men serving time in the stockade.
During that time, he also pursued a bachelor's degree. For eight years he
worked the graveyard shift as a toll collector on the Bay Bridge while taking
history classes at San Francisco State University (SFSU). One day he received a letter from the SFSU history department. He was only a few credits-
shy of a Master's degree. Would he like to join the graduate program? He
joined the program, continued on to the University of California San Diego
for his doctorate, and eventually took a position at Marymount College in
Los Angeles. Years after he had left San Francisco, he found a job announce-
ment in his campus mailbox with a note attached. It advertised an interdisciplinary program in social and behavioral sciences at the newest California
State University located on the former Fort Ord. The accompanying note
from a colleague read, "you should apply for this job." Shenk continues the
story:

> I read the job description and I said, you know this is the craziest job descrip-
> tion I've ever read. And I think I might just be the only historian in the country
> that has everything they're asking for. . . . What I saw in the description of
> CSUMB was an institution that was just beginning and that, at least on paper,
> reflected all of the latest scholarship on teaching and learning in higher educa-
> tion, but also really committed to a set of values that attracted me . . . I was
> very excited about coming here and about the fact that this was a conversion
> of, as Leon Panetta said, of swords to plowshares. [15]

The state of the campus tempered his excitement. "This place looked like a
desert. I mean the army had abandoned these buildings and they were in very
bad shape. I was brought to this building, which had paint peeling off. These

were just bare concrete floors. . . . It was an extremely depressing place to look at, in May of 1996."[16] He stayed for twenty years. For eight of those years, until his retirement, he represented the faculty on the board of the Fort Ord Alumni Association (FOAA), a joint veteran-university organization dedicated to preserving the Fort's history and providing student scholarships.

Shenk's story has an especially elegant arc. It opens with him visiting Fort Ord to advocate for and commune with soldiers, follows a circuitous path through graduate school, and turns back to the campus and to partnership with veterans. Like the abandoned army files turned into archives, Shenk's past experience with soldiers at Fort Ord became a significant if accidental feature of the university. His was a strangely appropriate fit, just as he predicted it would be when he first read the job description.

The circumstantial connection between Fort Ord and CSUMB is so extraordinary in this case that it would be easy to see Shenk's work with veterans as more serendipitous than inventive. Such an impression is due in part to the challenge of reconciling personal biographical details—his work with soldiers—with standard academic credentials and the usual professional narrative. Were it not for the notable coincidence of having occurred on the same campus, for instance, Shenk's prior experience with the military might have no academic significance at all. If, however, we treat circumstantial conditions as the very stuff of education, we find that such accessory and ancillary details play a more generative role in academic work than conventional narratives allow. From that perspective, Shenk's story is more representative than remarkable. Similarly curious and unexpected details play significant roles in stories from other faculty including the one-off experience, the local connection, the resemblances between ruptures, and events that relate if only because they happened in the same lifetime.

Complicated, Interlocking Systems

The story of how Joli Sandoz came to teach at Evergreen bears some resemblance to Shenk's. Her various life experiences also contributed directly if unexpectedly to her work at Evergreen. Sandoz has taught at Evergreen since 1995. Years before, in 1971, she was accepted into Evergreen's first cohort. She declined and instead attended school outside the state of Washington where she had grown up. "I'd wanted to go to grad school and at that time there were questions about whether the unusual education [at Evergreen] would be accepted by grad schools. So, I chose a more traditional route."[17] That might have been her only contact with Evergreen had it not been for personal circumstance. "I grew up near here and one of the people who was an adult in my life was on the first Evergreen Board of Trustees. So I kept in touch."[18] Sandoz returned to the Northwest years later. By then she had earned an unusual mix of degrees. Her studies were a good match with

Evergreen's interdisciplinary curriculum. The college's openness to creative disciplinary pairings made space for an academic career like hers. Even so, the strangely appropriate fit between Evergreen and Sandoz is the result of the work she has done to articulate her different interests. That is no small feat given how eclectic they are. Here she describes how she acquired degrees in literature and recreational education before attending seminary.

> I majored as an undergraduate in British literature and American literature just because I was interested in it. . . . But then I wanted to become a track coach after my experience of being on the track team at Portland State. So I earned a degree in recreation education. . . . And then after teaching and coaching at Fairmont State College and Humboldt State University for three years, I realized coaching is a very intense relationship with other people that I wanted to continue, but maybe in a different context. So I thought that becoming a minister would be a way to do that [and] . . . so went to seminary. I returned to coaching after graduation, choosing not to be ordained. [19]

Evergreen originally hired Sandoz to teach gay and lesbian studies because she also had experience as an LGBT advocate and journalist. She has since co-taught in interdisciplinary courses organized around issues in public health, sports, board game design, gender studies, literature, writing, and religion. When I met with her, she was team teaching in a program on sacred music titled "Amazing Grace" and preparing another program for the following academic year titled "Building Resilient Communities." She and her co-instructor planned to look at wealth and inequity. An activity Sandoz had completed twice as part of her recreation education degree inspired the course. "We physically walked around small towns and assessed park land in relationship to the population. We surveyed people in the communities about what they wanted from a parks and recreation department."[20] That experience, she went on to explain, was the basis for the connection between resilience and wealth that she hoped to make. "I'm pushing for us to think about the leisure studies aspect, or the leisure aspects of people's time and lives . . . Olympia [Washington] provides relatively few acres of park land compared to the number of people who live in this area. So, I'm hoping that will be part of our investigations."[21] Her prior experience working for the Washington State Department of Health and her fourth degree, an M.F.A. in Creative Writing, also had some influence on the course design. "We're going to include literature as one way of visioning and thinking about our lives."[22] The course on sacred music would provide further material. "I taught last night about how the first social movements in the United States were religious. . . . There are at least three main ways Americans talk about community. And each has roots in religion, so I'll probably talk some about that in 'Building Resilient Communities'."[23]

It was not her objective in planning "Building Resilient Communities" to link all of her experiences together. "I think to teach effectively about communities," she explained, "you have to teach them as complicated and interlocking systems with many diverse ambitions and lives."[24] Pairing land surveys with literature, leisure studies, and a discussion of spirituality was one possible configuration. Her hope was that students would become engaged in "the actualities of it" by first looking at their own lives and eventually moving toward the study of other people's communities.[25] Along the way, other design elements might come into play and shape the trajectory of the course. Sandoz teaches, for instance, in Evergreen's evening and weekends program "which sometimes draws more adult students and working students."[26] Both she and her co-instructor "come from a background similar to many of our students."[27] She anticipated that the personal details would direct their study of community life as much as any planned academic materials.

Like Shenk's path from and back to Fort Ord, Sandoz's background seems exceptionally well suited to her current position. To attribute that fit solely to her background, however, is like attributing to coincidence the match between an octopus and the rocky crag in which it sleeps. Sandoz's fit with Evergreen stems from her deliberate efforts to forge coherence between her eclectic background and the college's unusual approach to course design. Her background "fit" because she saw in the Evergreen seminar multiple ways of combining her life experiences and expertise. Like Shenk, Sandoz is more representative than not. Other faculty have crafted a fit for themselves in similar fashions.

The story of how a person comes to work at a particular campus and teaches a particular topic can seem logical and linear in the truncated form that appears on the curriculum vitae. The actual routes are rarely so linear in their long-form version. The longer narratives often meander along makeshift routes some of which all but disappear behind the person as they move. It is hard to imagine a place for those kinds of inventive movements in a permanent and timeless version of education. Such a model might still allow for people to bring life experiences to their work. Instruction might still take unusual forms. At its core, however, the search for seamless forms of education minimizes the hard work of wayfinding and diminishes the significance of possibilities both pursued and lost.

The Art of the Directional

Martha Henderson is a geographer and the director of Evergreen's Master's in Environmental Study. The story of how she came to Evergreen is a study in movement. She was born in Duluth, Minnesota, raised in Prineville, Oregon, attended school in Washington, Indiana, and Louisiana, and studied in Greece on a Fulbright before taking a job at the University of Minnesota at

Duluth. When I asked her how she came to Evergreen, she cited place as the main reason:

> Well, to be honest I just wanted to get back to the Northwest, back to the West. You know I'd been born in Duluth, I'd been raised on the north shore, I knew that whole Minnesota, northern culture, you know, I could speak Minnesotan pretty easily, you know, and I kind of railed against it all when I went there. [28]

Like Shenk and Sandoz, Henderson's story has her returning to a place—Duluth—with which she had a personal connection. As she tells it, having been raised on the north shore allowed her to fit in. While at Duluth, she was promoted—another, internal move. Unlike Shenk and Sandoz, those were not connections she wanted. For personal and professional reasons, she decided to move on. "I was an associate professor, I played the game. I worked really really really hard and I did everything you were suppose to do. I had a lot of publications." [29] Her interest in feminist studies allowed her to see her institutional positionality in something other than geographical terms. "I could see that I was the only woman in the geography department. . . . I did everything really well so it was really easy for them to say, okay well, we'll just leave Martha with these two hundred to three hundred classes . . . and I really railed against that." [30] When she picks up the narrative at a later point, she notes again the additional, personal, reason she had for moving. "And so there wasn't enough to keep me there and then on the other hand I wanted to get out west." [31] At this point in her story, another thread emerges and she adds a colleague's story as a complement to her own. She pairs the two stories because, as she notes, they contain an odd inversion. "Now I applied for two jobs and a colleague of mine from LSU applied for the same two jobs. He loves sailing. I love rodeos, because I come from Prineville. We both applied for the two [geography] jobs in the state of Washington . . . and he got the job at Central Washington and I got the job here and we've often reflected that the reverse would have been good for both of us." [32] As Henderson tells it, even though she accomplished her goal of returning to the west, she saw other possible connections—her love of rodeos; her childhood in Prineville—that would have made the position at Central Washington a better fit. She finishes the story by connecting it to more immediate events. "And a year ago I came *that close* to being hired as the chair over at Central; so, you know," she laughed, "I've learned to accept that I'm just never going to make it there." [33]

Shenk saw in CSUMB an excellent fit between his training as a historian, his commitments to critical pedagogy and the university's emergent interest in interdisciplinarity and social justice. Henderson, in contrast, describes her relationship to Evergreen as more of a mismatch. Shenk recognized his own pedagogical, political, and academic commitments in CSUMB's mission and vision. Henderson describes her relationship to Evergreen in geographical terms. By her own admission, she had "no idea how different Evergreen was."[34] Unlike Shenk, she was not drawn to the campus by something recognizable and familiar. To illustrate just how murky was her sense of Evergreen before she arrived, she relays a vague memory of having once visited the campus in the 1970s while enrolled as an undergraduate at Seattle Pacific. "I knew that it was really different. I think when I was very young . . . I think, once, I was here [at Evergreen], when they were sitting in a circle saying 'we're going to build the farmhouse'."[35]

Because Evergreen was so different from the campus she left behind and because she did not immediately identify with the project underway, she cast a wider net in search of a fit. Like the historians who scavenged through the abandon buildings at CSUMB, her own sense of curiosity proved generative. "I think that I always had a bit of curiosity" about the college, she explained.[36] While teaching at the University of Minnesota Duluth (UMD), she had connected with a regional sensibility and with the academic ethos that valued volume of productivity, an ethos she had acquired from her graduate training. "[At UMD,] I knew which classes I was going to teach. I knew what my textbooks were. I knew the politics of the department—all of that traditional college stuff.[37] To connect with Evergreen's alternative culture, she had to look to other life experiences.

> I'd spent a lot of time working for the forest service doing temporary work, living in the woods. I knew a lot of alternative people. And I taught environmental ed a lot before I got a graduate degree so when I got here I was like, this looks like advanced outdoor school. [laughs] And I could see there were well meaning people here. And I didn't mind the sense of alternative education.[38]

Those connections proved enough, although she found over time a need to revise her impressions of Evergreen as her feelings shifted. "You move into a very different world at Evergreen. And . . . unless you work at it, it can be pretty insular; it gets to be its own little bubble."[39] At several points, she described her relationship to Evergreen in terms of eastern and western Washington and Oregon, two regions divided by the Cascade Mountains with notably different climates and different political affiliations. "I've come to see that I can be that sort of central Oregon conservative person, too, at a very fundamental level about individual responsibility."[40] Here again she refers to regional differences to mark the misalignment she feels.

Her eastern Washington-orientation generated some dissonance in her relationship to Evergreen. It also inspired a course on exploration that she designed and co-taught. In the spring quarter of the yearlong program, Henderson offered students the opportunity to explore the state of Washington by walking across it, east to west, beginning at the Idaho border and ending on the other side of the Cascade Mountains. The project, she explained, was about power, transference, and transformation, threads that Henderson pulled through multiple aspects of the curriculum. As Henderson explains, the first act of transference was to shift responsibility for the course from herself onto her students.

> I never carried a map on that thing. Now, we were on a trail, right. [laughs] It was very well defined! You don't need one. [But] the students were responsible for planning it. So it was that transfer of power from me as the person of power to them as the people who in the end confiscated my coffee pot and told me when we were getting up.[41]

As the class walked the state, they saw other manifestations of power and examples of transference. They inhabited landscapes defined by agricultural industry in some instances and by hydropower in others. The remnants of past landscapes—a defunct railroad—promised multiple archives including history of the Pacific tea trade and of Chinese laborers. Henderson explained other thematic connections:

> But the other part of the power transformation, thinking about the geography of the Northwest, is, of course we're walking from Idaho to beyond the crest of the Cascades on the west side—and you walk through a landscape that's been totally transformed for power. Now this was when hydropower was the most visible form of power on the landscape, this was in 2000. And now you'd walk through that same landscape and you'd be overwhelmed by wind power, turbines all over the place. So there's been you know a transformation of the Washington landscape to one that's seen as *really* a power production site.[42]

At the end of her account, Henderson made one more deft transition, this time from academic insight to practical consideration about the prospect of writing a book about the walk. The transition she makes from reflective to practical concerns is nearly seamless. She concludes her reflections about the walk and its significance, and then in the next sentence we are in the present moment again, as indicated by her reference to the unfinished manuscript. "We're so segmented, compartmentalized in our lives and our experiences and our knowledge to the point where we're powerless. And so to me, hopefully finishing that manuscript is about how we tell a story."[43]

Henderson's description of the project showcases the kind of compositional ingenuity for which academics are known. Her walk across Washington offers an alternative to the vision of unbounded education idealized in the University of Everywhere. It is at odds with a vision in which education is realized through a progressive series of pre-existing forms. The walk across Washington instead approached teaching and learning as an iterative, inventive practice shaped by select details. A handful of students participated in a resource-intensive, one-time course that exposed them to a specific sociopolitical and natural environment. It was a singular project. It resided in the individual steps that Henderson and students took in a specific academic year. Were she to undertake it again, it would be an altogether different project due to environmental and social changes in the landscape and the new considerations its observers might bring. In that alternative vision, education goes in one direction to avoid another. It takes a circuitous route, occasionally loses its way, sometimes dead ends, and often circles back to a starting place only to find that the beginning looks nothing like it did before.

Coordinated Movements

I asked Henderson what for her was most vivid about Evergreen. "We kept the light on," she replied. "It's the fact that we kept the light on in a dark world."[44] Her choice of words brings to mind the common association between light and wisdom. Taken in a more literal sense, it speaks to the materiality of education and the routine maintenance involved in running a college. Her response resonates with the story about the students at CSUMB who moved closer to the windows because their classroom had gone dark. Both that story and Henderson's comment associate education with basic institutional maintenance. Alongside academia's grander gestures are classrooms with desks, windows, electricity, and the class schedule someone has made. Education emerges from the coordination of those materials, not the existence of information. It is coordination that lends durability to the educational movements described previously.

The last two stories in this chapter illustrate the relationship between movement and coordination in the work of education. The first story tells about a faculty member who contributed to the design of Evergreen's newest building. The second is about the CSUMB professor who schedules the science classes each semester. The first story ends with a grand addition. The second tells of more mundane and repetitive work. In a conventional account, only one of these projects might be considered generative and durable. The other might be characterized as administrative upkeep. I present them side-by-side to highlight their resemblances and to suggest that education emerges from the interplay between the two different kinds of work. Both exemplify the economical, well-positioned, timely, and flexible movements that the ancient Greeks honored with the notion of mêtis and that distinguish institutionalized education from its unbounded forms. Both involve choices made, options eliminated, inventive arrangements, and a pairing of generalizable and local knowledge. Both contribute, on different scales, to the continuous reconstitution of educational spaces and practices.

A Moment That Went on for Quite Awhile

Buildings exemplify the kind of enduring legacy that educational institutions hope to make. Rob Knapp's contribution to Sem II is such a legacy, but even more notable is how his contribution came about. His story illustrates the extent to which being in the right place at the right time has more to do with skill and ingenuity than simple luck. It illustrates, too, the extent to which education is a matter of mobilizing possibilities.

Seminar Building II, otherwise known as "Sem II," was finished in 2004. It is the second addition to Evergreen's campus since the 1970s. Like the veteran's alumni organization at CSUMB, it is a fitting addition to the college. Giant windows fill the LEED Gold certified space with views of the same forest that Richard Nichols believed made Evergreen. The building minimizes impact on local salmon runs with a rooftop garden and embedded concrete flows that funnel runoff into underground holding tanks, a splendid solution to the drainage problems Nichols noted in 1972. The classrooms can accommodate a range of class sizes, just as Edward Shoben proposed in 1969.

Ask Knapp, a professor emeritus at Evergreen, to tell the story of Sem II and he will begin with the energy crisis in the 1970s. A physicist by training, Knapp joined the Evergreen faculty in 1972. He designed and co-taught the "Technospheres" program in 1974, which looked at local energy production. "And a colleague of mine," he explained, "proposed a brilliant, classic Evergreen program called 'Energy Systems' that was going to be about technology and politics of energy."[45] Over the years, Evergreen faculty ran multiple iterations of "Energy Systems." Knapp attributes his interest in energy efficiency to this peculiar historical moment in which the momentum of a new college propelled an ongoing response to a national energy crisis.

> The pattern at Evergreen is to rotate teaching. You don't just lock into one thing and teach it year after year after year. You review the curriculum every year and . . . you may return to something you've taught, but you're not going to just do it over and over and over again. So I was part of the rotation to do "Energy Systems" and it was a lively program with a lovely topical and challenging subject matter.[46]

Knapp continued to teach programs with an energy component. "I learned more and more about energy and I turned out to be particularly interested in energy saving; not the big machines that produce it but . . . the clever ways of not needing it. That appealed to me. I think I'm a sail boat person rather than a power boat person, if just temperamentally."[47]

The story picks up three decades later when, he explained, "there came a moment that went on for quite a while." Then a seasoned faculty member, Knapp carried into that moment years of teaching and administrative experience along with his knowledge of green energy, all know-how on which he drew when an opportunity presented itself. "I did another tour of duty," he continued, "in the late nineties as a dean. . . . And at that moment I became aware that Evergreen was about to build its first classroom building in a long time and I was the one person probably on campus that knew that *and* knew there was such a thing as a green building. Other people knew about green buildings. Other people knew about the project. But I knew both."[48] Knapp seized the moment. When an architect joined the faculty, Knapp teamed up with him to offer a course in green buildings. He consulted his colleagues in the social sciences on the human dimensions of spatial design. He involved students in the project. In one related activity, students toured a green building in Canada and learned about compost toilets. They returned to campus excited to pitch the idea. They failed to convince the building designers, but, as Knapp explained, the proposal pushed the bounds of possibility such that otherwise "radical" ideas made the cut.[49]

Sem II stands as a testament to Evergreen's interdisciplinarity, commitment to sustainability, and its educational ethos. The building is a centerpiece in the daily life of the campus. It houses faculty offices each personalized with fliers and cartoons. Classes meet and rearrange the modular walls, desks, and chairs to better suit their needs. The light in the rooms changes throughout the day and from one season to the next, as does the landscape beyond the windows. The building is finished, and it is constantly in motion. It is a living manifestation of the cyclical approach to education first articulated by the faculty when the college opened. As Knapp describes it, a rhythmic institutional work led to Sem II's features. That work involved course and administrative rotations that continued year after year: Different faculty cycled in and out of the "Energy Systems" seminar teaching a curriculum that both repeated and gradually changed course; Knapp did "another tour of duty" as dean. Those activities gradually wore grooves in the campus and eventually materialized in Sem II's design. The building offers visible evidence of old campus routines. It is supported by other, less visible rhythms. The final story in this chapter surfaces that essential support work. Even when facilities are new; even when all the lights work, someone still needs to coordinate the activities that assembly people in classrooms.

Keeping the Lights On

The campus had very little infrastructure when Sharon Anderson joined the CSUMB faculty two years after the university opened. "That was way back in the old days when everything was by the seat of the pants here."[50] The founding faculty were learning in those early years all that goes into running a college, including the importance of coordinating schedules. That activity took on newfound significance after everyone attempted to make their own schedules the first year only to realize that it would not work to run every single class on Tuesdays at 10:00 in the morning. Anderson stepped into the project underway at CSUMB after leaving what she described as "a functional well established R1."[51] Her story bears some resemblance to Henderson's. "I'd been on the research treadmill for long enough to know that I didn't like having graduate students and post docs with brand new babies dependent on me for their pay check. I was good at getting money but it wasn't money to do stuff that I wanted to do," she explained.[52] Attracted by the prospect of helping launch a new university, she left Michigan and moved west. "I think I liked the idea of service learning even though I didn't understand it then. And I liked the idea of working with . . . the farm worker communities . . . I'd lived a year in Mexico and my husband is Mexican and . . . it was just really that mission of serving the historically underserved."[53]

The lack of facilities was a notable difference between CSUMB and the campus she left behind. In Michigan, she had "a 3,500 square foot research lab. And [at CSUMB], you know, [in] the teaching labs, if you plugged in all the hot plates at once in the chemistry lab, the circuit breaker blew."[54] The lack of lab facilities was one thing, but the campus also lacked fundamental infrastructure. "This building wasn't here. The library wasn't here. There were falling down buildings all over campus. There was no grass on the quad."[55] The physics faculty taught their first class in the parking lot of an elementary school. The absence of "ego maniacs," she said, was also notable. "Some people were a bit into building their empire, but they were doing it for the students," Anderson explained. "That was the most amazing thing."[56]

That same spirit, she suggested, has carried through the years even if the energy of the university's founding faculty has waned. "We were all really young when we started here." Now decades into the project, Anderson's work patterns have changed. "I can't pull these all-nighters for the university."[57] A former department chair, dean, and department vice chair, Anderson remains involved in the day-to-day upkeep of the campus, including hiring, advising, and course scheduling. "I kind of oversee our advising and . . . I probably do about, I don't know, twenty or twenty-five hours of advising appointments a week, when it's prime time, and then I kind of have to cut back and catch up on all my other stuff for awhile."[58] Anderson has also done the course scheduling for the science classes since 1998. She had no prior experience when she took over the task. Her description of how the responsibility developed and how she learned to manage it echoes the creative making-do in Knapp, Henderson, Sandoz, and Shenk's stories. "You know, the detailed stuff like the course scheduling, that's not—for someone who is use to looking at large data sets, it's not hard. It's like a puzzle, like any of the other puzzles that I work with. So, that wasn't hard to figure out. Actually, it's fun. It kind of forces me to go around and check in with all the faculty."[59]

Anderson's contributions share key qualities with those of Knapp: both are born of knowing the right details at the right time, and both reflect the institutional rhythms they helped to establish. Anderson's flair for scheduling is all the more impressive when you learn that multiple colleagues have tried their hand at it.

> A couple of chairs have wanted to get involved in the scheduling and I've kind of handed it off to them and tried to give them my institutional knowledge but it's kind of a huge mess just because there's specific lab spaces for specific courses and some need fans and some need certain equipment and the amount of time to transfer all that knowledge is longer than most people want to invest.[60]

Anderson's knowledge of the schedule led in turn to her advising more students. "I'll know two semesters out what's going to be offered at what time and whether there's going to be a time conflict. And so, it kind of started with, 'oh go see Sharon because she'll make sure that those classes you're planning to take your last semester won't conflict.' And then it just got bigger."[61] Anderson's administrative role grew in part from her first-hand knowledge of all the details that went into running a university. It requires classroom spaces, electricity for the hotplates, coordination of faculty and students, and knowing which subjects need which kind of facilities and which majors need which courses in which sequence. "And so," Anderson explained, "trying to come up with times that work with the faculty, that work with the fact that you need this class in daylight, and this person, a single mom with small kids, . . . can't teach at night . . . it's this big huge puzzle."[62]

When asked what she likes about the work she does, Anderson spoke to the importance of coordination at a more fundamental level. "For me," she said, "it's all about getting students to realize that they are going to leave here with a college education and that puts them in a really elite group even if they're the 'C' student that's just scrapping by. *And there's a whole lot of things that had to fall into place for them to be able to get that college education* even if . . . you know, even if they didn't think about it. We have students, you know, with all kinds of stories [emphasis added]."[63] Her comment speaks to the critical force behind all the selecting, assembling and arranging that goes into education. In the case of CSUMB, that work established a campus in the middle of an underserved area and made it possible for students to go to school and stay close to home; it shaped a campus in the image of its surrounding communities making it possible for people to see themselves in the institution. It intervened in the social routines that discouraged or prevented many people from attending college. Pieces came together in ways they had not before.

Anderson offered another example of CSUMB's interventions when she described a service-learning course she had designed. The course illustrates the degree to which education is a matter of coordination, and how that work can contribute to new social routines. The course places CSUMB students in a local high school as science tutors. The students in her class "see the kids that can't afford the five bucks for the science lab fee. Their parents are paying it in one dollar installments over five weeks or something [and] it's just eye opening for them."[64] They also see an old elementary school repurposed as a high school (a history that resembles their own campus), and they see the difference a box of Kleenex and pipe cleaners can make to a lesson in DNA molecules. They help to organize that space and those materials, just as Anderson has done on their campus. For the high school students who work with CSUMB tutors, a whole lot of things fall into place that might not otherwise as the campus rhythms ripple outward.

Strangely Appropriate

According to an army training manual found in an abandoned filing cabinet, teaching is creating the conditions under which learning may occur. When we can see the work that goes into creating those conditions, the question of what education should be proves less interesting than the question of what it could be. Of all the variables at play in a high school science class, for instance, which are proper to Anderson's service-learning course? The structure of DNA? Pipe cleaners? Students' family finances? The unusual structure of a service-learning course lends visibility to the range of possibilities. The trick is not to lose sight of such questions when we turn away from alternative campuses like CSUMB and Evergreen and look at more traditional institutions. The breadth of possibility is no less present. A heightened visibility is the main difference between alternative campuses and other colleges and universities. Sometimes the familiarity of the answers obscure the questions, as happens when science is reserved for science classes held in science buildings. Even then, the decisions that lead to such arrangements are no less convoluted or arbitrary than their alternative counterparts.

Education is a selective process no matter the subject or underlying philosophy. It is also an inventive process. Its critical edge lies in the ability to see possibilities in different combinations of elements. The stories presented here showcase the inventiveness with which faculty have undertaken that work. Moreover, they give us a sense of what to look for if we wish to see inventiveness underway at other institutions. The history of higher education in the U.S. is full of such activity, although the lowly status of teaching often prevents it from being recognized as a rigorous form of knowledge-production in its own right. The next chapter looks back at the inventiveness that structured earlier eras of the American college system. The stories shared previously are an extension of those long-standing traditions. When paired with past practices, they dispel an impression of higher education as hopelessly incoherent. Repeating questions and reoccurring debates appear less like a state of confusion and appear instead to be the rhythmic responses that gradually shape and re-make educational projects again and again.

NOTES

1. Gerald E. Shenk, "Requiem for a Vision in Higher Education," Unpublished manuscript (Seaside, CA: September 2014).

2. Ibid., 19.

3. Joseph Gabriela, "A Vision of the Future: Painting the New Face of CSUMB," *Otter Realm* (September 18, 2014): 9; Stephanie Anne Johnson, "Toward a Celebratory and Liberating System of Teaching Public Art," *The Practice of Public Art*, Eds. Cameron Cartiere and Shelly Willis (New York: Routledge, 2008). The campus, for instance, has made some efforts to salvage the murals it inherited from the army base and to include military history in its public art. A 2001 Visual Public Art (VPA) class repurposed one mural at the intersection of Inter-Garrison and 5th Avenues that contained military motifs and lead paint. A second VPA class in 2014 replaced the mural all together. The first VPA project, *The Windows Project*, was initiated by muralist Judith F. Baca and implemented by the VPA program founding faculty Johanna Poethig. Students painted onto the windows of abandoned barracks the portraits of soldiers (real and imagined) who may have served at Fort Ord.

4. Noah Remnick, "Yale Grapples with Ties to Slavery in a Debate Over a College's Name," *The New York Times* (September 11, 2015): http://www.nytimes.com/2015/09/12/nyre-gion/yale-in-debate-over-calhoun-college-grapples-with-ties-to-slavery.html?_r=0. Recent debates over the names of dorms, for instance, have drawn the charge that such myopic diversions distract from more substantive social problems.

5. Dwight Conquergood, "Rethinking Ethnography: Towards a Critical Cultural Politics," *Communication Monographs* 58 (1991): 184.

6. Jean and John Comaroff, "Ethnography on an Awkward Scale," *Ethnography* 4, no. 2 (2003): 170.

7. Peter Simonson, "Reinventing Invention, Again," *Rhetoric Society Quarterly* 44, no. 4 (2014): 317.

8. Janet Atwill, *Rhetoric Reclaimed: Aristotle and the Liberal Arts Tradition* (Ithaca, NY: Cornell University Press, 1998). In a survey of Greek literature, Atwill surfaces definitions of techne that associate the term with mêtis, kairos, topoi, and topographical images of alternative paths and roads.

9. Atwill, *Rhetoric Reclaimed*, 70.

10. Jay Dolmage, "'Breathe Upon Us an Even Flame': Hephaestus, History, and the Body of Rhetoric," *Rhetoric Review* 25, no. 2 (2006): 212.

11. Debra Hawhee, *Bodily Arts: Rhetoric and Athletics in Ancient Greece* (Austin: University of Texas Press, 2004), 47.

12. Hawhee, *Bodily Arts*, 56. The octopus, along with the fox, is the animal figure for *mêtis* in Ancient Greek myth and it appears in literature, Hawhee explains, as "a figure of cunning polymorphousness" that "suggests a modality of response constantly bound up in its flexible, adaptive movement between things."

13. James C. Scott, *Seeing Like a State: How Certain Schemes to Improve the Human Condition Have Failed* (New Haven, CT: Yale University Press, 1998), 316; Hawhee, *Bodily Arts*, 48.

14. Eric Charles White, *Kaironomia: On the Will to Invent Ithaca* (New York: Cornell University, 1987), 160; Michelle Ballif, "Writing the Third-Sophistic Cyborg: Periphrasis on an [In]Tense Rhetoric," *Rhetoric Society Quarterly* 28, no. 4 (1998): 65.

15. Gerald Shenk (CSUMB faculty in the Division of Social, Behavioral, and Global Studies) in conversation with the author (Seaside, CA: October 10, 2014).

16. Ibid.

17. Joli Sandoz (Evergreen faculty) in conversation with the author (Olympia, WA: April 25, 2013).

18. Ibid.

19. Ibid.

20. Ibid.

21. Ibid.

22. Ibid.

23. Ibid.

24. Ibid.

25. Ibid.

26. Ibid.

27. Ibid.

28. Martha Henderson (Evergreen faculty and Director of Evergreen's Master of Environmental Study program) in conversation with the author (Olympia, WA: April 22, 2013).

29. Ibid.

30. Ibid.

31. Ibid.

32. Ibid.

33. Ibid.

34. Ibid.

35. Ibid.

36. Ibid.

37. Ibid.

38. Ibid.

39. Ibid.

40. Ibid.

41. Ibid.

42. Ibid.

43. Ibid.

44. Ibid.

45. Rob Knapp (Evergreen faculty emeritus and former Academic Dean) in conversation with the author (Berkeley, CA: February 28, 2013).

46. Ibid.

47. Ibid.

48. Ibid.

49. Author's field notes (Olympia, WA: April 25, 2013).

50. Sharon Anderson (CSUMB faculty and vice-chair in the Division of Science and Environmental Policy) in conversation with the author (Seaside, CA: November 19, 2012).

51. Ibid.

52. Ibid.

53. Ibid.

54. Ibid.

55. Ibid.

56. Ibid.

57. Ibid.

58. Ibid.

59. Ibid.

60. Ibid.

61. Ibid.

62. Ibid.

63. Ibid.

64. Ibid.

Chapter Three

Invention's Scaffolding

Critics who fault higher education for institutional incoherence join a tradition that extends back to America's first college boom in the nineteen hundreds. It was then that the nation's college boosters first questioned whether higher education might serve a purpose other than religious conversion. Might it also offer civic preparation, unfettered inquiry, or professional training? The debates that ensued came to define higher education. In his 1936 memoir, Henry Seidel Canby described American colleges as exceptional in their disharmony. "[T]here has never been anything quite like the American college of the turn of the twentieth century, never any institution more confused in its purposes, more vital, more mixed in its ideals."[1] Robert Maynard Hutchins, writing that same year, also characterized higher education as consumed by its disagreements. "The most striking thing about higher education in America," he wrote, "is the confusion that besets it."[2] A famous quip attributed to Wallace Sayre offers a more contemptuous view of academia's penchant for discord: academic politics are so intense, the saying goes, because the stakes are so low.[3] Sayre cuts deeper than Canby or Hutchins by characterizing higher education as lacking in substance as well as coherence.

Academia's reputation for superficial discord stems in part from the piecemeal fashion in which higher education emerged in the United States. It initially developed as a collection of independent campuses oriented toward local circumstance. Its disjointed, cloistered quality was a geographical fact before it was an institutional fault. Colleges bore little resemblance to one another and had negligible reason to interact. An educational system emerged only after campuses began sharing more attributes and embraced similar administrative and organizational patterns. They adopted professional conventions, recognized one another's degrees, and faculty formed independent associations that transcended institutional affiliations. Those changes brought a sense of coherence to academia, and yet, the more coherent higher education became, the harder it was to see the generative relationship between specific teaching and inquiry practices and distinct institutional forms. As system-wide conventions took hold, the particular features that distinguished one campus from another gradually appeared inconsequential. Systemic coherence obscured substantive discussion about what counted as knowledge, who should access it, and how best to organize that work.

That so many colleges and universities adopted similar forms deepens the impression that higher education in its early years merely suffered from confusion. The current hierarchical system of tiers and rankings perpetuates the sense that institutional differences signal little more than mastery or deficiency in a proven model. During the nineteenth-century college boom, however, different approaches to organizing circumstance were worthwhile achievements in their own right. Colleges and universities were not comparable to one another at that time, but neither were they confused about what they wanted to be. They were curious about what was possible. During a period spanning approximately 1850 to 1900, the institutions now known as Ivy League, research, land grant, regional, or liberal art first took shape or else experimented with approaches.[4] Educators sought new ways to define and distinguish their campuses and to organize their work. Roger L. Geiger describes it as "a distinct era" that saw a "proliferation of colleges at nearly as rapid a rate as student enrollments."[5] Lawrence R. Veysey adds that both established and new institutions alike enjoyed "the luxury of widespread public indifference" which "permitted . . . a variety of abstract conceptions of the university to blossom."[6] Three distinct approaches to emerge from that time illustrate how organizational and administrative instruments once served as purposeful design achievements in education. The course elective adopted at Harvard allowed students' individual pursuits to shape the direction of their studies. The Wisconsin Idea developed at the University of Wisconsin (UW) extended the campus to the state's borders, and Clark University first experimented with research expectations that have since become conventional benchmarks of success. The early proponents of these ideas saw institutional form as central to their projects, not a distraction from it. Charles W. Elliot, president of Harvard, John Bascom, president of the University of Wisconsin, and G. Stanley Hall, president of Clark University, all spoke of the need to manage the possibilities that academia presented by placing parameters on education and inquiry. The elective course at Harvard, the Wisconsin Idea, and the organization of research culture each did so on different terms. Collectively, they expanded higher education's domain even while they appeared philosophically incompatible.

The early iterations of these three approaches gave no reason to assume they would become enduring educational forms. Their acceptance into mainstream educational discourse secured their place in history, but it did not dispel the sense that higher education suffered from dysfunction. Even today their critics continue to dismiss them as additional noise in higher education's cacophony, but the three have proven historically compatible, if philosophically at odds. That alone is an accomplishment. The historical narrative that finds higher education burdened by confusion misses the eloquent ways in which these projects have lived side by side since their emergence from the nineteenth-century college boom. They remain both contested and accepted in part because they do not cancel each other out. Each designated a register of knowledge not apparent in the others. Their distinct contributions have allowed them to co-exist and even to take up residence in modified form within the same institution.

The neighborly spirit of these organizational approaches invites a different story about higher education, one that finds its institutional forms more relational than conflicted. Higher education's iterative, mutable, and relational qualities are all features of invention.[7] Institutional inconsistencies that we attribute to a clash of ideas are invention's rhythmic motions. Considered in those terms, colleges and universities no longer appear as imperfect answers to philosophical questions. They appear instead as inventional circuits that generate what John Mucklebaur calls "singular rhythms."[8] Elliot, Bascom, and Hall set possibilities in motion. Their ideas continue to reverberate throughout higher education. Years later, CSUMB and Evergreen modified pieces of those projects and further expanded higher education's field of vision. After briefly revisiting the nineteenth-century college boom, this chapter looks at how Elliot, Bascom, and Hall arranged education and inquiry and then follows the threads of those projects in CSUMB's Service Learning Institute and Evergreen's Native Pathways Program and its contributions to Native American and World Indigenous Peoples Studies.

When Every College Was Experimental

The first U.S. college boom generated diversity in institutional design akin to that celebrated by the Carnegie Council in the 1970s. Edward Shils notes that the first iteration of an academic system in the U.S. "had no center" and "no hierarchy."[9] Colleges and universities were sovereign and isolated from one another. Christopher Jencks and David Riesman believe that colleges may have cultivated localism "to induce a comparatively underdeveloped nation to support something as apparently superfluous as higher learning."[10] Either way, Shils describes the result as "an amorphous agglomeration of institutions and activities . . . not only scant in number and widely dispersed territorially but the connections between them . . . infrequent and of marginal importance."[11] Even the first land grant colleges, established with the passage of the 1862 Morrill Act, kept the local orientation of their predecessors.

Roger L. Williams describes each as having been "uniquely determined by a complex set of conditions and circumstances within its respective state."[12]

Early nineteenth-century American higher education was religious in mission and rigid in character. Colleges offered mental and moral discipline. Students trained in daily classroom drills to tame their faculties while the isolated and rule-bound academic life was thought to shepherd religious conversion. In the second half of the nineteenth century, colleges began to articulate different missions with an eye to teacher education, science, engineering, agriculture, and commerce. It was not uncommon for campuses to combine philosophies and morph into what Geiger calls the "multipurpose college."[13] For instance, even though the denominational college continued to dominate higher education, it no longer strictly resembled the "'oldtime' classical college."[14] Many colleges introduced new curriculum while continuing to instruct students in mental gymnastics and promote a Christian life.

The invention of the American research university and the concomitant rise of academic professionalism produced profound changes eventually transforming a collection of disparate and scattered experiments into a loosely associated and disjointed system. Research culture and academic professionalism influenced higher education in two ways: Academics began to see themselves as knowledge producers rather than mere guardians of established knowledge, and research universities fostered professional networks that transcended individual campuses. Faculty began to identify with a discipline as they might an occupation. Educational reform efforts developed in and through changing notions of scientific inquiry and a desire for knowledge that was comprehensive in addition to being true. Motivated by a progressive conception of science, educators wanted responsive institutions and curricula, not static monuments to accumulated facts. Those developments shared a commitment to open inquiry and a dream of limitless education and endless inquiry. At its founding in 1868, Cornell University adopted the motto: "an institution where any person can find instruction in any study."[15] Frederick A. P. Barnard, president of Columbia, defined the university in his 1882 annual report as having "no definite limit at all."[16] No longer bound by religious obligations or regional student populations, the emergent research university embraced the notion of boundless knowledge and adopted general professional protocols that superseded their local identities.[17] Colleges and universities still established a locality and conducted their work locally, but academics now conceptualized higher education's terrain along professional as well as geographical lines.[18]

American universities borrowed the notion of pure research from the German universities but then established their own "institutional condition[s] for its cultivation."[19] The sciences led these changes by forming professional associations for the purposes of circulating research and credentialing fields of study. Academia's various and competing interests in cultural inculcation, scientific exploration, and emergent industry eventually "transformed local-ized, avocational circles of learning into a highly differentiated business of professional knowledge production."[20] The first American doctorates and the advent of the academic journal contributed key elements to that communica-tion infrastructure.[21] The hiring of one department's doctorate by another, for instance, established a new kind of connection between campuses. Scholars no longer worked independently in isolation. Research gained visibility as it moved from the private study and laboratory into the college and university. The development of schools within universities "revealed not only special-ization but strivings for programmatic coherence and academic and public visibility."[22] Research institutions gradually sought to distance themselves from their regional associations and even the idea of regionalism. New media technologies aided this effort. The same publishing infrastructure that ushered in regular periodicals "helped to transform the very idea of learning and culture from . . . universal truths to . . . an evolving, ever improving body of information and knowledge about the real world."[23] Academics likewise began to cultivate what Shils calls a "translocal identification" constituted through "a vast, national and international movement."[24]

The professionalization of inquiry also impacted teaching. Where once the pedagogical goal had been to master traditional bodies of thought, pro-grams now prepared students for the indefinite pursuit of specialized re-search, a mission that required a re-orientation to knowledge itself. Daniel C. Gilman, president of Johns Hopkins University from 1875 to 1901, cited this new expansive mission when touting his university's pioneering academic journals. The purpose of publishing, he explained, was to "extend the useful-ness of [Johns Hopkins] far beyond the company of those whom we constantly instruct."[25] That ambition was aided by the nineteenth-century revolution in print culture, which offered new publishing technologies and which saw the emergence of "middlebrow" reading publics.[26] Those new technologies brought what Burton J. Bledstein calls a "riot of words" into American homes and raised fears about whom and what to trust.[27] Academ-ics were among the professionals who offered expert guidance through this expanse of new fields.

The advent of professionalism and the expansion of academic networks led colleges to look for additional ways to identify and classify students. Many campuses justified exclusionary and discriminatory practices by pro-moting intangible qualities like aptitude, drive and ability. The belief that such qualities could be determined and education formulated to students' individual abilities shaped higher education's overall design.[28] Teaching, agricultural, and community colleges opened for the purpose of populating specific professions and to differentiate students by their suitability for vari-ous types of professions. Other stipulations imposed for the purpose of main-taining the existing social stratification, such as "separate but equal" clauses, also fueled the growth in colleges. [29] The Morrill Act of 1890 included such a clause, which prompted the founding of the first public colleges for Black students.

Higher education's first flood of institutional activity courted a sense of disorder by demonstrating that education and inquiry could be organized along countless lines. Its different structures destabilized traditional knowledge less by challenging it than by supplementing it and inviting space for the unknown. Academic administration became an exercise in imagining how a stationary institution could advance into the vast territories of inquiry and then compose a coherent account of the known world. The administrative instruments that colleges and universities devised sometimes demonstrated the futility of the effort. Colleges and universities could not replicate the world in miniature. They could only establish select conditions and parameters for education and inquiry, and even that project came with seemingly endless variables. Three administrative instruments—the course elective, the Wisconsin Idea, and the research faculty position—give a sense of the variables and possibilities at play. All three are accepted practice today, but their origin stories show them as once arbitrary and seemingly superficial organizational ideas. When first introduced, they had no more valid claim than anything attempted at Evergreen or CSUMB.

Education's Infinite Complexity

When Charles W. Eliot assumed the Harvard presidency in 1869, he inherited what Richard C. Levin characterized as a parochial institution. [30] Harvard hosted schools of law, divinity, and medicine alongside an undergraduate college. Its school of science, its first foray into America's nascent research culture, competed with the undergraduate college for laboratory space. [31] Eliot wrote an article for the *Atlantic* a few months before he was inaugurated in which he signaled discontent with higher education's organization. He prefaced his criticism with an exhaustive description of the science programs or "nonclassical" degrees offered at Harvard and eight other campuses. Compared to the undergraduate colleges, this "new system of education," he says at the outset, is "crude, ill-organized, and in good degree experimental." [32] To show the diversity of approaches, he surveys the physical resources, requirements and requisites for admission, the composition and employment arrangements of the faculty, instructional approaches, length and course of study (including use of exams and field trips), course sequencing, and number of graduates at each campus. His discussion of the Columbia School of Mines gives a sense of level of detail that he reached. He noted in that case the number of professors and assistants employed (eight and four), the number of students enrolled (eighty-nine), and how many of those students followed a "regular course of instruction." [33]

Eliot did not conduct his exhaustive survey to affirm the classical liberal education defended in the 1828 Yale Report, which advocated a "prescribed" curriculum designed with the intent of "awakening, elevating, and controlling the imagination."[34] He instead found fault with programs that combined a prescribed course of study with loose admission requirements (e.g., accepting students as young as fourteen). That approach, he argued, served neither practical nor academic aims. In a challenge to the liberal curriculum, he advocated a broad and open course of study for mature students. He was not alone in his support for electives. President Barnard of Columbia University (1864 to 1889), "believed that 'the educational problem of the day' was to discover how to shape colleges and universities that would meet the demands of a modern, industrial society" and he "promoted electives as the first step toward building an 'encyclopedic' university."[35]

Though Eliot does not mention the course elective, the organizational formula that he espouses in the *Atlantic* shares the same philosophy that he later cites in defense of it. His vision of the American university stemmed from two related beliefs, both articulated in the *Atlantic* article.[36] First was his belief that "no subject of human inquiry can be out of place in the programme of a real university" (n.p.). Knowledge had an infinite horizon and pursuit of it should not be prescribed. His second belief explains how an institution might then organize an advance on the knowledge horizon. He believed that a "division of mental labor" was "essential in civilized communities in order that knowledge may grow and society improve" (n.p.). As Veysey explains, this organizational scheme "moved the individual to the center of the educational universe and boldly asserted that all educated men need not know the same things."[37]

For Eliot, the inclinations of each individual mind lent a natural structure to the endless quest for knowledge, or as he put it in his inaugural address, "the individual traits of different minds have not been sufficiently attended to."[38] Eliot saw an organic limit on education in individual self-governance.[39] In thinking about how those natural limits worked, Eliot advanced what he called "a mechanical argument."[40] No one individual, he explained, possessed the capacity to absorb all the lessons offered at a university at a given time. "A diligent student," he argued, "would need about forty years to cover the present field; and during those years the field would enlarge quite beyond his powers of occupation."[41] Since narrow and prescribed curricula were both impractical and "intolerable," the only workable course of action was to allow students to self select their studies.[42] Eliot presented the elective as an educational and organizational necessity, so much so that it he spoke of it first in the broad vision of the university that he presented in his inaugural address. It distinguished the university from the college and the lower grades; it dispensed with secondary curricular questions that Eliot believed to be misguided and settled the central question of any curricular dispute: what

should a student learn? That Harvard had instituted a "tolerably broad elective system" before he became president bolstered his case. Just a year into
his presidency, the campus arranged its course catalog "by field rather than
by class of students who were allowed to take them."[43]

A belief in the individuality of each person and respect for self-governance formed the twin pillars of Eliot's organizational approach to education.
About the first he wrote: "Every youth of eighteen is an infinitely complex
organization, the duplicate of which neither does nor ever will exist."[44] Colleges could access the possibilities by granting students the freedom to self-
direct: the "university must permit its students, in the main, to govern themselves."[45] His assurance that an "elective system does not mean liberty to do
nothing" foreshadows the arguments made by President McCann at Evergreen nearly a hundred years later.[46] Neither wished to give their audiences
the impression that a college without walls was a college without structure.
For his part, Eliot saw the college freshman as a microcosm of the college
campus; both reflected the "infinite variety of form and feature" that situation
and circumstance generated.[47] Like the variety of academic institutions that
dotted the U.S. landscape, individual students would, by dint of their personal pursuits, impose order onto possibility.

The course elective proved a contentious idea and many administrators
lamented the headaches it introduced into the college catalog. Reuben attributes their concerns to a fear of fragmentation in the academic project and the
sense that the elective could not be reconciled with the notion of holistic
education and cohesive knowledge. The elective favored individualism and
special interest over development of the whole student; an elective-driven
curriculum, Reuben explains, "no longer recapitulated the whole chain of
knowledge."[48] The elective did more than complicate the liberal arts. It presumed that every campus and program had limitations. That premise raised
the question of what a campus should aspire to be if it could not encapsulate
the world.

The State as College Campus

The question of what a campus could be was especially resonant for emergent land grant universities such as UW that lacked the financial resources its
eastern peers enjoyed. UW's organizational approach illustrates the interplay
between the era's educational philosophies, which more often conjoined at
the institutional level than triumphed over one another. In place of students'
individual pursuits, the university chose the state's borders as the parameters
of its knowledge project. The particular way in which it resolved the tensions
between open-ended research and specialized application was the hallmark
of its approach. Eliot saw a resolution for these competing pursuits in the
passions and inspirations of individual students whom, he believed, could

organically divide up the labor of knowing the world. UW divided the labor geographically. A 1909 editorial by Lincoln Steffens explains the main difference between the two approaches: one defined the university as a place where "anybody may learn anything" while the other was a university "reaching for these people" by "offering to teach anybody—anything—anywhere."[49] The UW pursued the latter by symbolically extending the campus across the entire state. The university then oriented research activities to regional affairs and public problems.[50] The state thus became a "laboratory" with inquiry aimed at bettering society. The Morrill Acts had set the stage for the geographical organization of education, but the Wisconsin Idea as it became known showed the potential for specialized research domains to be as arbitrary as a location on a map. CSUMB's regional mission is the distant outgrowth of that approach.

The Wisconsin Idea was an educational model, an advisory body, and a research outlet.[51] It started as extension programs and a series of Farmer's Institutes that developed in response to requests for help from the dairy farmers. By 1910, over five thousand people were enrolled in correspondence courses and district extension centers opened all over the state.[52] The university also opened a Bureau of General Welfare (an information center with emphasis on agricultural topics) and a Bureau of Debating and Public Discussion, which sponsored local discussion groups and provided a traveling lending library.[53] A university-government partnership was a second component of the Wisconsin Idea. UW lent its expertise by placing professors on commissions to assist with legislation. Over forty faculty members were serving on state commissions by 1907 and helped to enact some of the most progressive legislation in U.S. history.[54] Wisconsin's 1911 legislature limited the working hours of women and children, created the nation's first worker's compensation program, created industry and highway commissions, established conservation programs for water and forests, created a state life insurance program, and strengthened farm cooperatives.[55]

Jack Stark attributes the Wisconsin Idea to the same experimental spirit that Eliot saw in the new science colleges.[56] A series of university figures contributed to it. Charles McCarthy gave it a name, but many credit John Bascom for its philosophical foundation.[57] Bascom served as president of UW from 1874 to 1887 and during that time articulated a vision of the state's obligations to its citizens, the university's obligations to the state, and the individual's obligations to both. Inquiry and public service conjoined in his vision of the land grant university. He cited Christian principles as warrants for his arguments, but grounded his notion of service in academia's emergent research culture.[58] Bascom believed the pursuit of ideas should be unrestrained and its "horizon clear."[59] Even his description of religious instruction reconciled traditional doctrine with the "dynamic, plastic" truths that modern inquiry generated.[60] Such instruction, he counseled, should reveal

"the complex world" and "enable us to see how this world accepts the doc-
trines brought to it, expounds, modifies, and combines them."[61] He opposed
instruction "narrowed down to a single dogmatic system and he opposed
restrictive college admissions for the same reason: both risked "narrowing
dogma."[62] If education was to serve a common good, he argued, it needed to
be an open project. His vision of a university working toward the betterment
of society thus combined religious moralism, utilitarianism, and empiricism
into a "living" and "fluid" philosophy.[63]

Both Eliot and Bascom favored opening higher education beyond its established and narrow liberal arts curriculum. Their visions diverged in the
administrative details. In an 1877 commencement address "Education and
the State," Bascom offered a forceful defense of public education and advanced a rationale for expanding admissions. Eliot had argued for restricting
admissions, if only by age, and allowing maturity to direct students' pursuits.
Bascom saw educational glory in "broad foundations" and "large-hearted
emulation."[64] His goal was to establish "a sacred enclosure of public sentiment . . . beyond the invasion of private interests" and to secure the "common
grounds of advantage."[65] But the university would not realize its potential, he
suggested, if it relied on voluntary participation motivated by personal gain.
The state should not wait for students to go to college, but should instead "lay
hold of its own wealth by taxation [and] build for its motley population
common and sufficient institutions."[66] The university, in turn, had to work in
and through the state's citizens to unite "all interests in one large and liberal
work."[67] It was the duty of government, he believed, to "provide those common conditions . . . which lie beyond the reach of individual and corporate
action."[68] Citizens in turn had a duty to the state. "You have no right," he
told the graduating class of 1877, "to seek your own weal, if your own weal
does not include the public weal."[69] He likewise counseled Wisconsin farmers (the first group to benefit from UW's outreach and extension programs)
against isolating themselves with protectionist policies. He urged them to
join the professional classes, embrace science, and contribute to a better
society.[70]

Bascom elaborated the mutually influential relationship he envisioned
between the individual, the state, the university, and Christian ideals in his
last commencement address at UW in 1887. Bascom's vision nearly inverts
Eliot's in which the individual is a microcosm of the university each limited
by material constraints like time and attention. Where Eliot trusted individual
pursuits to shape the course of academic study, Bascom condemned unbri-
dled individualism as a threat to a greater good. He credited individualism for
social ills that included regressive forms of taxation, financial speculation,
corporate monopolies, the consolidation of wealth, and use of alcohol, all of
which he characterized as forms of social erosion. Individual and institutional interests align in both his and Eliot's visions, but for Bascom, the Christian

state would be founded in the harmony between voices that spoke to "one passion" and "one inspiration."[71] Eliot espoused the course elective as a virtuous instrument of self-governance. Bascom saw a higher virtue in the belief of "thy neighbor as thyself."[72] Since he also believed that individual and state interests aligned, it followed for him that the state held "the right and duty to push to completion its own organization."[73] From that premise, Bascom addressed the 1887 UW graduates as servants of the state. They have, he told them, "enjoyed, not only the protection of the state, but its aid, bestowed in a very extended and liberal form."[74] Bascom's successors continued that project and UW gradually organized the state of Wisconsin, person by person, into a campus.[75]

The Endless Frontier

The Wisconsin Idea emerged alongside a research culture that did not share UW's regional commitments. Departments defined by disciplinary specialization were not beholden to the state. Disciplinary associations established domains of knowledge, not geographical boundaries. Modern research culture accelerated with the publication of Vannevar Bush's 1945 report *Science, the Endless Frontier*. The federally commissioned report channeled the new enthusiasm for scientific research that grew out of wartime efforts and expressed the hope for a postwar economy fueled by "new and better and cheaper products."[76] The report called for a national research foundation and for greater recognition of the nation's universities as the engines of research. Academic institutions should be the ones, Bush argued, to "expand the basic scientific frontiers."[77] His proposals stemmed from the belief that research required the right kind of institutional support for boundless possibility. "Discoveries," he wrote, "come from remote and unexpected sources" and the processes of inquiry could not be prescribed.[78] Professional norms redirected faculty energy away from the kinds of civic projects and public policy that UW undertook.[79]

By the time he issued his report, the generative role in unfettered research that Bush envisioned for universities had been a work in progress for over half a century. Its first iterations were as experimental as any other aspect of the emergent U.S. university.[80] At the helm of one of the nation's first universities dedicated to research, G. Stanley Hall grappled with the question of how to access the limitless prospects of inquiry through an institution's limited infrastructure. Before Hall, Gilman championed the university as an organized advance into the unknown. He pioneered sustained research at the University of California (UC) and Johns Hopkins and popularized the idea that research required dedicated infrastructure such as instruments of measurement, observation, and experimentation. Inquiry required, he explained in an address to UC Berkeley, "walls which shall furnish homes to . . . collections of books, maps and charts, and works of art, museums of geology and natural history and archaeology, laboratories for chemical, physical, botanical and zoological researches [and lenses] for the microscope and the telescope."[81] Gilman characterized academic infrastructure as necessary to a world that was "a great laboratory, in which human society is busy experimenting."[82] He believed universities offered a superior means by which to organize and disseminate new knowledge because they were free of the capricious and arbitrary impositions that shaped other institutions. The university, Gilman argued, "has been wider than the boundaries of any state; their citizens have not been restricted to any one vocabulary; their acquisitions have not been hid in [a] crypt."[83] Under his direction, Johns Hopkins served as a hub through which learned minds passed and from which research disseminated through the nation's first academic journals.

When Hall assumed the presidency at Clark after leaving Johns Hopkins, he sought to refine Gilman's vision of the research university. Gilman aspired to build the German research university alongside the U.S. college. Hall set out to reconcile the two forms in service to inquiry. Before starting at Clark, he negotiated a yearlong leave of absence and arranged a "pedagogical tour" through Europe to see first-hand everything from laboratories to administrative methods.[84] When he returned, he launched the first postgraduate campus in the country designed to operate with a "true mental freedom which no amount of acquisition can bring."[85] Hall's vision distilled the research university down to a few features that he hoped to then nurture into excellence. Clark opened without an undergraduate college and admitted a handful of graduate students.[86] It hosted only five areas of study: mathematics, chemistry, physics, biology, and psychology. The campus supported a small faculty recruited with generous salaries and the expectation that they would dedicate themselves to research exclusively. Students worked alongside professors as research partners. This arrangement cleaved research from education and relieved faculty of traditional teaching obligations by transforming instruction into a research activity.

Hall's organizational approach broke from both the teaching college and the grand sweeping university to give "special prominence" to original research.[87] He troubled the assumption that universities must represent the world or cultivate the whole student. "We must not attempt at once to cover the entire field of human knowledge," he cautioned.[88] "Each science has become so vast and manifold that it is impossible to cultivate the frontier of all at a single university."[89] Like Eliot, Hall saw little to gain in trying to imitate other campuses or replicate the same education for each student; he proposed instead that institutions "freely differentiate."[90] Hall's innovation was to bring the institution in scale with inquiry practices, which did not proceed from grand gestures but through pursuit of a few careful projects undertaken by close attention to minutia.

The benefits of the small and precise, including the close contact between the professors and students, was a theme in his annual reports and in his editorials. In his first report to Clark's trustees, he argues that "research cannot be successful with large numbers."[91] He goes on to describe laboratories outfitted, journeys undertaken, methods found, animals preserved, drawings done, observations recorded, artifacts collected, literature organized, and material "sifted and arranged."[92] Hall conveyed a sense of grandeur by sharing the specifics of faculty projects, which ranged in subject from minerals in Arkansas to the nature of rhythm. He offered a glimpse into inquiry's vast expanse with a survey of the details. The studies underway included "the petrography of the State; chemical action as affected by electricity in the field of a strong magnet; the crystal structure of isomorphous compounds . . . a standard of length in terms of a light-wave one fifty-thousand of an inch long . . . studies of sea-anemone and jelly-fishes; the breeding-habits and embryology of the lobster . . . [and] the myths, customs, and beliefs of the native Indian tribes of British Columbia."[93] The list had enormous breadth, but Hall shared it to show the "care of things small as well as great."[94] The small things included the storage of a metal bar used to establish a "single unalterable standard" that had to be "carefully guarded in a vault."[95]

Hall expounded on his vision of research in the *Pedagogical Seminary*, the journal that accompanied his program in "higher pedagogy" that he founded at Clark during his presidency.[96] His inaugural editorial and subsequent essays affirmed his belief that individualism and specialization offered a superior means of organizing inquiry.[97] He believed that general culture, the focus of liberal arts programs, posed an obstacle to research. It stymied the very kind of differentiation that Hall sought in comparative studies and that he promoted in educational administration. "The products of a too prolonged general culture are among the saddest products of our contemporary institutions," he argued.[98] Even while a general course of study promised a unified experience, in practice it broke knowledge "into standardized units of hours, weeks, terms, credits, blocking every short cut for superior minds and making a bureaucracy which represses personal initiative and legitimate ambition."[99] Hall so opposed a general approach to academic work that he recommended idiosyncrasies be "not only tolerated but respected and perhaps welcomed."[100] Academic glory lay in small and careful undertakings that proceeded without a clear destination or timeline. Hall had enormous faith that his colleagues and students would eventually produce something, and "we cannot wonder," he advised, "that men are content to labor long and obscurely to bring one new stone to an edifice so magnificent."[101] Even while he attributed the drive for new knowledge to a natural spirit, he dedicated his tenure at Clark to securing the institutional conditions that made lengthy esoteric research possible.

Singular Rhythms

As colleges and universities gradually embraced similar approaches to education and inquiry and familiar forms emerged, critics no longer saw institutional differences as signs of confusion or conflict. Those differences appeared instead as deficiencies, imperfections, or evidence of inferiority. [102] By the time Evergreen and were founded, higher education was divided into tiers that measured schools in areas like research productivity. A campus could perform well or poorly by those measures and their performance defined their relationship to other schools. The idea that each school might be valuable in its own right as a unique site of education and inquiry was remote and difficult to defend. Faculty at Evergreen and CSUMB nevertheless founded campuses in the spirit of that idea. Both feature aspects of Eliot's course elective, Bascom's regional orientation, and Hall's research culture. A metric like research productivity misses the ways in which Evergreen and CSUMB have extended the inventional circuits that Eliot, Bascom, and Hall forged. When viewed as an extension rather than a version of another institution, Evergreen and CSUMB's contributions resemble an earlier era of campuses. Each expanded higher education's field of vision by further modifying domains of knowledge and then building the infrastructure to actualize those domains. CSUMB's Service Learning Institute and Evergreen's Native Pathways Program and Native American and World Indigenous Peoples Studies exemplify that work.

Decisions made at the federal and state level and a change in CSU leadership set CSUMB on an unusual path. The idea of founding a university at the former Fort Ord materialized only after interested parties cast about for other economic development options. [103] Donald Gerth describes CSUMB as "a product of politics at a very high level." [104] The opportunity to secure a large swath of acreage along California's central coast and replace a military base with a viable employer overrode state protocols for founding new campuses. The potential benefits to the local economy, and not a sense of unmet educational needs, drove the project. [105] No one made a case for a CSU campus in Monterey County prior to the closure of Fort Ord. [106] Once the idea hatched, the regional community in Monterey and Salinas envisioned a public university that would take advantage of local opportunities in the marine sciences, languages, and the arts. [107] The momentum to transform Fort Ord into a university benefited from a 1989 California legislative report that took stock of the state's institutional models, and from the appointment of Barry Munitz as chancellor of the CSU system. [108] Both the 1989 report and Munitz supported a change in the educational approaches enshrined in California's Master Plan for Higher Education. Munitz agreed that the CSU should attempt "a 'break the mold' campus that would pioneer new visions of what 21st century education would look like." [109]

Invited to be nontraditional, CSUMB founding faculty departed from the organizational design outlined in California's master plan.[110] Faculty sought to make research an integrated and routine feature of the university. The early stages of planning included some talk of a partnership with the University of California, which would have enabled the campus to develop traditional research programs.[111] That partnership never materialized, but the faculty nevertheless broke from the teaching mission assigned to it by the state and designated the new campus a site of knowledge production. They did so by forging a close relationship between instruction and inquiry and, like University of Wisconsin, attributing value to regional research. The university's vision statement articulates this interest where it promises to "strive for distinction, building on regional assets in developing specialty clusters."[112]

CSUMB had embraced regionalism as a core value before constraints at the campus also made it the most practical option for future inquiry. The faculty had a year to prepare for the first incoming class and no funding for research space or equipment. It was not enough time to draft a course schedule let alone fundraise, renovate, or slowly and carefully pursue a specialized area of research. Twelve faculty members worked out of a single story building alongside the admissions office. They had all accepted positions as professors of interdisciplinary studies and agreed to come to a university with no departments, programs, dorms, offices, or curriculum. Their appointments led to responsibilities and projects that were in some cases far afield of the work they had done before. When Marsha Moroh arrived on the campus, someone said to her "you won't believe all of the things that haven't been done. You ask a question about where the policy on so and so [is], and there isn't one. And so not only has it not been done, but if you want it done, you have to do it yourself."[113] Moroh described the sense of freedom the project afforded and the frustration it generated. "When you're operating a university, when you do the schedule, they say, here are the blocks. You put your courses in. Here are the courses, you put these courses in those blocks. But just think about trying to do the schedule where you haven't made up the courses yet and there are no time blocks."[114]

CSUMB faculty worked creatively within these organizational and material constraints. One way they did so was to reframe regionalism as another type of research specialization. Doing so elevated regional research to the same status as a subfield, which is always narrow and arbitrary in scope. Such was the approach of the Fort Ord Watershed Restoration Demonstration Project, which presumed a global interest in restoring and understanding California's central coast ecology. A 1994 funding proposal submitted to the Department of Defense articulated the national value of watershed restoration by connecting it to the regional impact it promised. The project, which is now the Watershed Institute, relayed its distinctiveness by foregrounding local ecological and demographical details. Faculty did not consider this level of specialization to be a limiting factor. Like any research project, its niche contribution was its strength. In addition to offering "a major work-based learning program" and "a remarkable outdoor classroom for decades of science education," its authors promised the project would also be "a national model for positive environmental action." [115]

CSUMB's program in visual and public arts illustrates a second approach to regional research. [116] In this case, faculty argued regional context and positionality as relevant to all research. Muralist Judith Baca and performance artist Suzanne Lacy, both founding faculty, drafted the 1995 vision for the program, which was the first of its kind. They drew from public art traditions that treated site-specific work as a defining feature of the art form. In a move reminiscent of Hall's criticism of general culture, the program presumed context and placement to be defining features of all art. "At CSUMB," they explained, "the making of visual art is not separable from a consideration of its context. Because of this, we build a significant portion of our curriculum for the first five years around an extended public art project housed within the Institute for Public Art, The Fort Ord Conversion Project. We take the land on which this college sits as our starting point . . . and [through] our curricular and extra-curricular projects we excavate this site for meaning." [117]

These two approaches to regional research came together in CSUMB's service learning program. Like the watershed project and the public art program, service learning at CSUMB valued specialized knowledge and appreciated positionality as relevant to all research. Unlike Hall's Clark University, CSUMB elected to extend inquiry opportunities to undergraduates and embed service learning in its lower-division requirements as well as requiring it in the major. That model challenged the belief that the lower division served only to prepare students to participate in inquiry processes at a "higher" level of study. [118] CSUMB thus modified specialized research by extending two of Hall's arguments to service learning: inquiry should be free to explore any aspect of the world, and even the smallest contributions should be taken seriously.

Similar to the Wisconsin Idea, service learning expanded the campus boundaries to the entire tri-county region. The prospect of a university contributing directly to local organizations was attractive given that CSUMB started as a federal initiative that promised to replace the Fort. Whole areas of the local economy disappeared when Fort Ord closed. Seth Pollack who directs CSUMB's Service Learning Institute explained the benefits of service learning from a community perspective. Many people from surrounding cities had worked at the base. "There was a real connectivity," Pollack explained, and "there was a desire for a university to continue and contribute in that way." [119] A 1993 regional survey conducted by Marian Penn indicated that 95 percent of local organizations "saw a need for student interns and volunteers in their programs."[120] Service learning at CSUMB benefited from the National Community Service Trust Act, President Bill Clinton's first piece of legislation. The bill established the Corporation of National Service and earmarked funding for a handful of projects. CSUMB was one of the first recipients. Leon Panetta, Clinton's chief of staff and former congressional representative for California's 17th district (which encompassed Monterey County) provided the connective tissue between this national funding mechanism and local communities.

To ensure that service learning received the institutional support that it would require, CSUMB established the Service Learning Institute, a decision that elevated service learning by equating it with the twenty other academic units on campus all of which started as "institutes" rather than departments. It was not, Pollack explained, "just an administrative support unit."[121] What many saw as a pedagogical practice was positioned at CSUMB as an area of study akin to visual arts or wetlands science. As it was explained in CSUMB's first self-study, this decision "positioned [it] as an 'institutional-ized' academic identity—not simply a good idea in the university's residential life center or a component of individual courses offered by a handful of committed faculty members."[122] The study goes on to note that CSUMB's commitment of resources was "innovative on the national scene."[123] Its level of internal programming and regional outreach were unusual. In 1995, the university surveyed 1,200 regional nonprofits and government agencies and built a database from the 350 responses it received. The Institute developed an advisory board, hired outreach coordinators, provided assistance to faculty teaching service learning courses, and trained students to serve as ambassadors. Faculty appointed to the Institute were expected to conduct related research and stay abreast of related literature.

The invitation to contribute both instruction and scholarship set the stage for recognizing service learning as a specialized knowledge that in turn generated specialized knowledge. Pollack was attracted to the inquiry opportunities the Institute presented. Penn had served as the first director of service learning at CSUMB and established the Institute. When she left, Pollack was hired to direct the Institute in 1997. That same year he earned his doctorate from Stanford University and coordinated a federal grant that brought together four universities—Stanford, Portland State University, Mills College, and CSUMB—that shared an interest in strengthening their community-university partnerships. That work brought him to CSUMB at a time when Pollack was not interested in pursing an academic career. "I thought maybe I'd work for a foundation or some sort of research place, or some sort of community development organization."[124] He knew from his visits that the university wanted service learning to become a central feature of its curriculum. Inspired by that prospect, he submitted a last minute, against-the-odds application and got the job.

The prospect of building a service learning program appealed to Pollack who served as a Peace Corps volunteer for five years in Mali prior to pursuing graduate work. Pollack's position in Mali influenced his thinking about academic-community partnerships. "The most valuable thing Peace Corps is able to give," he explained, is a "really rich, grounded, situated awareness."[125] His experience with international organizations offered a lesson in one model of service.

> I was at the heart of the development tourist model. I saw one expert after another from Germany and from the Netherlands and from France and from America and from Russia come over and kind of just be experts. . . . I watched how disconnected that was from the reality of the lives and the cultures and the economics and just the integrity of the communities that I was in. . . . You go watch this stuff come in and touch down in such a de-centered way that you know this stuff is not going to last.[126]

Pollack left that experience disillusioned and struggling to understand why localized knowledge was so "disrespected and seen as unimportant."[127] In opening a space to engage that question, service learning at CSUMB generated a form of critique. It surfaced old debates about how to distinguish research from teaching, the proper scope of inquiry, and the value of its detail, context, and place. The point of reviving those debates was not to settle them (e.g., whether expertise is more valuable than local know-how).[128] The point was to offer different answers to reoccurring educational questions. Pollack, for instance, has argued that service learning is "not just a technique to teach," but rather "a content" and "a knowledge base."[129] Like any area of study, it generates its own internal body of expertise that in turn can be used to generate additional forms of scholarship.

Remapping the Endless Frontier

Like the regional projects undertaken at CSUMB, Evergreen's Native Pathways Program (NPP) and Native American and World Indigenous Peoples Studies (NAWIPS) revived reoccurring questions about what counts as knowledge and who can participate in its formation. One of the responses to those questions came in the form of the opening of Evergreen's "House of Welcome" Longhouse Education and Cultural Center in 1997, the first academic building added to the campus since the 1970s. Evergreen had offered indigenous studies since its first academic year, but the Longhouse raised its visibility and deepened its commitment. As one Evergreen faculty member explained, the building was "an acknowledgment that indigenous knowledge is on par, is equal to and is as important as other kinds of knowledge."[130]

The year that Evergreen dedicated the Longhouse, there were twenty-nine identified American Indian colleges in the U.S., most of them two-year programs.[131] Most scholarship about Native and Indigenous peoples still came from disciplines such as anthropology or linguistics. The absence of disciplines at Evergreen, its willingness to let student interests shape the curriculum (part of the legacy of the course elective), and what one faculty member described as its "free-wheeling kind of flat organization" left space at the college for indigenous studies and educational programs to form.[132] Evergreen's regional mission laid the groundwork for partnering with Northwest Native nations and tribes. The Quinault Indian Nation and the Squaxin Island, Makah, and Skokomish tribes all contributed to the construction of the Longhouse and when the idea emerged to offer an extension program at neighboring reservations, the college's existing policies and practices supported doing so. The college already had infrastructure in place that enabled curricular modifications of the kind that made the NPP workable. Evergreen's Evening and Weekend program, for instance, had established protocols for students who wished to enroll part time, a practice made difficult by the structure of the Evergreen seminar. The college's long tradition of independent studies and its recognition of prior learning as equivalent to formal education meant that Evergreen had administrative instruments on hand, such as independent studies contracts, to support a program that incorporated Indigenous pedagogies, methodologies, authorities, and cultural resources. These were essential institutional conditions for students who did not wish to leave the reservations on which they lived and who wished to pursue "a liberal arts degree from a native perspective."[133] Barbara Smith, Evergreen's former provost, cited the importance of geography and regional partnerships in launching the NPP.[134] Evergreen worked with neighboring community colleges and Northwest Indian College, Washington's only tribal college, to connect with students who were completing lower-division courses and wished to continue with upper-division work. Prior partnerships with these campuses had introduced ideas and practices to Evergreen that would prove important for the NPP, such as having faculty travel to students to hold classes.[135]

Evergreen had a ready-made infrastructure that it adapted for the NPP. Instructors and students then pursued additional modifications to traditional course work and inquiry practices as the NPP took shape. These modifications were necessary, explained one member of the faculty, because students had the sense that they were earning two degrees in one. "They're [learning] the basics and plus they have to learn what's happening in Indian Country."[136] For instance, questions arose about the purpose of following certain research protocols. If students had no interest in using mainstream research networks, as was the case with an oral history project that now resides in a Quinault archive, were instruments like human subjects review and standardized citation still useful or appropriate? Even where those instruments proved worthwhile to learn, their purpose or role might require additional clarification about whom they safeguarded and what they legitimated.

Topics relevant to Pacific Rim first nations and tribes and answers to those questions filtered back to Evergreen's main campus and helped shape the college's NAWIPS offerings which are open to all students. Zoltan Grossman taught a representative seminar with Laura Evans called "Conceptualizing Native Place" in which students visited with the Nisqually tribe and documented a number of projects including a salmon hatchery on former reservation lands that flow through what is now Fort Lewis military base. That student research, Grossman explained, was possible only because the seminar provided space to prepare students in the research protocols and ethics of working with and alongside Native communities.

Grossman first became interested in teaching at Evergreen after hearing about a student partnership with Native peoples to research and protect a burial ground of the Yakama Nation located at Lyle Point in the Columbia River Gorge. He was struck that students would forge such a partnership and contribute directly to the preservation effort "instead of just taking a detached view of the whole thing."[137] It became apparent to him that Evergreen did not generalize first nations nor were Native studies "subsumed within a larger context of ethnic studies, or a sidebar to environmental studies." It had "its own identity at the Longhouse" and many programs were specific to the region.[138] Evergreen's extension programs at neighboring reservations and its contributions to NAWIPS are two ways in which the campus has remapped higher education's historical landscape. The former resembles aspects of the Wisconsin Idea but draws attention to the ways in which state universities often fail to extend themselves to all people residing within their geographical service area. Likewise, NAWIPS's combination of regional and global perspective challenges the idea of the frontier as a stable space into which scholars advance. For Grossman, who worked as a professional cartographer before earning a doctorate in geography from the University of Wisconsin, the idea that inquiry has a single frontier does not resonate. The frontier, he explained, is as much about "destruction and detachment" as it is about "advancement and progress."[139] His is a perspective that acknowledges inquiry's inventive dimensions. "I think the interesting part," he added, "is how . . . the pieces are put back together."

He could be describing the ways that higher education has developed ever since it fractured during the first college boom. Those earlier educational experiments remain influential. Their continued presence has prevented higher education from settling into a coherent vision. Every campus wrestles with those earlier forms. But so long as we believe that higher education suffers from dysfunction, we will only ever see that work as more and less successful attempts to advance toward a single ideal. Evergreen and CSUMB have turned that historical project toward critical ends, not because they alone experiment, but because they stylize their work as experimental and alternative. Doing so helps to keep open the question of how else education might be arranged.

NOTES

1. Henry Seidel Canby, *Alma Mater: The Gothic Age of the American College* (New York: Farrar & Rinehart, 1936): viii.

2. Robert M. Hutchins, *The Higher Learning in America* (New Haven, CT: Yale University Press, 1936), 12.

3. Alan L. Otten, "Politics and People," *Wall Street Journal* (December 20, 1973): 14.

4. A decade after passage of the 1862 Morrill Act, twenty-four land grant institutions enrolled upwards of twenty thousand students. Williams, *Origins of Federal Support*, 40.

5. Roger L. Geiger, "The Era of Multipurpose Colleges in American Higher Education, 1850–1890," *The American College in the Nineteenth Century*. Ed. Roger L. Geiger (Nashville, TN: Vanderbilt University Press, 2000), 132.

6. Lawrence R. Veysey, *The Emergence of the American University* (Chicago: University of Chicago Press, 1965), 17.

7. Karen Burke LeFevre, *Invention as a Social Act* (Carbondale: Southern Illinois University Press, 1987); Louise Wetherbee Phelps, "Institutional Invention: (How) Is It Possible?" Ed. Janet M. Atwill and Janice M. Lauer *Perspectives on Rhetorical Invention* (Knoxville: The University of Tennessee Press, 2002): 64–95; Peter Simonson, "Reinventing Invention, Again." *Rhetoric Society Quarterly* 44.4 (2014): 299–322; Eric C. White, *Kaironomia: On the Will-to-Invent* (Ithaca, NY: Cornell University Press, 1987); Debra Hawhee, "Kairotic Encounters," Ed. Janet M. Atwill and Janice M. Lauer. *Perspectives on Rhetorical Invention* (Knoxville: The University of Tennessee Press, 2002), 16–35.

8. John Muckelbauer, *The Future of Invention: Rhetoric, Postmodernism, and the Problem of Change* (Albany: State University of New York Press, 2008), 33, 43.

9. Edward Shils, *The Order of Learning: Essays on the Contemporary University* (New Brunswick, NJ: Transaction Publishers, 1997), 30. Shils goes on to describe it in some detail: "There were governmental scientific bureaus and the bare beginnings of research in a few industrial enterprises; there were very few learned societies or associations, few scientific or scholarly journals; there was one national quasi-governmental academy . . . there were museums and a few large libraries and there were many universities and colleges."

10. Christopher Jencks and David Riesman, *The Academic Revolution* (Chicago: University of Chicago Press, 1968), 187.

11. Shils, *Order of Learning*, 30.

12. Roger L. Williams, *The Origins of Federal Support for Higher Education* (University Park, Pennsylvania, 1991), 41.

13. Geiger, "Era of Multipurpose Colleges," 131.

14. Ibid., 128.

15. Cornell University, *Annual Report to the Board of Trustees* (Ithaca, NY: 1881); Julie A. Reuben, *The Making of the Modern University: Intellectual Transformation and the Marginalization of Morality* (Chicago: University of Chicago Press, 1996).

16. Frederick A.P. Barnard, *Annual Report of the President* (New York: Columbia University Press, 1882), 30.

17. A notable exception to this was the agricultural research supported by the land grant institutions. The Hatch Experiment Station Act of 1887 furnished each state with federal annual appropriations for agricultural stations.

18. Jencks and Riesman, *The Academic Revolution*, 160. Jencks and Riseman attribute the loss of localism in higher education to the rise of academic professionalism. The growing emphasis on research made academia "inevitably cosmopolitan rather than local in outlook."

19. Shils, *Order of Learning*, 11.

20. Janice Radway, "Research Universities, Periodical Publication, and the Circulation of Professional Expertise: On the Significance of Middlebrow Authority," *Critical Inquiry* 31, no. 1 (2004): 209.

21. The federal government first began to recognize the benefits of research with passage of the Adams Act of 1906 which allocated each state $30,000 for "original" scientific research.

22. Hugh Hawkins, "University Identity: The Teaching and Research Functions," Eds. Alexandra Oleson, and John Voss, *The Organization of Knowledge in Modern America, 1860–1920* (Baltimore, MD: The Johns Hopkins University Press, 1979), 294.

23. Radway, "Research Universities," 220.

24. Shils, *Order of Learning*, 8.

25. Quoted in John Tebbell, *A History of Book Publishing in the United States*, 4 Volumes. (New York, 1975), 2:536; see also: Hugh Hawkins, *Pioneer: A History of the Johns Hopkins University, 1874–1889* (Ithaca, NY: Cornell University Press, 1960), 74.

26. Radway, "Research Universities," 225–26.

27. Burton J. Bledstein, *The Culture of Professionalism: The Middle Class and the Development of Higher Education in America* (New York, NY: W.W. Norton & Company, 1978), 78.

28. David L. Lewis, *W. E. B. Du Bois: Biography of a Race 1868–1919* (New York: Henry Holt and Co., 1993), 69–80. W.E.B. Du Bois's experience at Harvard University provides one such example of the kind of administrative instruments that colleges used to maintain social stratification along racial, gender, and class lines. Du Bois held a degree from Fisk University, a Black student-serving institution. Harvard did not recognize his degree from Fisk and Dubois earned a second bachelor's degree from Harvard before joining its graduate school.

29. James S. Coleman, "The Concept of Equality of Educational Opportunity." *Harvard Educational Review* 38, no. 1 (1968): 7–22.

30. Richard C. Levin, *The Worth of the University* (New Haven, CT: Yale University Press, 2013), 9.

31. Levin, *Worth of the University*, 8.

32. Charles W. Eliot, "The New Education: Its Organization," *The Atlantic* (February 1869): n.p.

33. Ibid.

34. https://www.thepublicdiscourse.com/2018/08/21589/.

35. Reuben, *The Making of the Modern University*, 61–62.

36. Reuben, *Making of the Modern University*, 66–67. Reuben adds that emergent research culture grew support for electives and development of scientific laboratories.

37. Veysey, *The Emergence of the American University*, 305.

38. Charles W. Eliot, "Inaugural Address as President of Harvard, 1869," *Educational Reform* (New York: The Century Co., 1898), 12.

39. Hazen C. Carpenter, "Emerson, Eliot, and the Elective System," *The New England Quarterly* 24, no. 1 (1951): 13–34. Hazen C. Carpenter draws a number of parallels between Eliot's arguments for the elective course and Emerson's views of education. Both entrusted the student with the power to direct their own individual course of study.

40. Charles, W. Elliot, "The Elective System: How to Transform a College with One Uniform Curriculum into a University" (1885): n.p. http://www.higher-ed.org/resources/Charles_Eliot.htm

41. Ibid.

42. Ibid.

43. Ibid.; Hawkins, "University Identity," 293. Harvard gradually abolished required studies. It first transformed the senior year into elective courses and eventually eliminated requirements in each preceding year.

44. Elliot, "The Elective System."

45. Ibid.

46. Ibid.

47. Ibid.

48. Reuben, *Making of the Modern University*, 230.

49. Lincoln Steffens, "Sending a State to College: What the University of Wisconsin is Doing for Its People," *The American Magazine* 67 (1909): 354.

50. David J. Hoeveler Jr., "The University and the Social Gospel: The Intellectual Origins of the 'Wisconsin Idea,'" *The Wisconsin Magazine of History* 59, no. 4 (1976): 282.

51. John F. Witte, "Wisconsin Ideas: The Continuing Role of the University in the State and Beyond," *New Directions for Higher Education* 112 (Winter 2000): 7–16.

52. Paul Westmeyer, *An Analytic History of American Higher Education* (Springfield, IL: Charles C. Thomas, 1997).

53. Ibid.

54. Hoeveler, "The University and the Social Gospel," 294. Westmeyer adds that by 1910 thirty-five professors were "assigned part time to various state commissions: political scientists helped draft legislation, university engineers helped to plan roads and buildings." Westmeyer, *An Analytic History*, 75–76.

55. Jack Stark, *The Wisconsin Idea: the University's Service to the State*. Reprinted from the 1995–1996 Wisconsin Blue Book (Madison, WI: Legislative Reference Bureau, 1995), 110–11.

56. Ibid.

57. Hoeveler, "University and the Social Gospel,"; Curti, *University of Wisconsin*.

58. Bascom taught a popular philosophy class while at UW in which he reconciled religion and science. Merle Curti, and Vernon Carstenson, *The University of Wisconsin: A History, 1848–1925, Volume 1* (Madison: University of Wisconsin Press, 1949), 278.

59. John Bascom, *Things Learned by Living* (New York and London: G.P. Putnam's Sons, The Knickerbocker Press, 1913), 116.

60. Hoeveler, "The University and the Social Gospel," 287.

61. Bascom, *Things Learned*, 141.

62. John Bascom, "Education and the State," Address given at the University of Wisconsin (June 17, 1877): 18.

63. Curti, *The University of Wisconsin*, 295.

64. Bascom, "Education and the State," 13.

65. Ibid., 17.

66. Ibid., 13.

67. Ibid., 19.

68. Ibid., 6.

69. Ibid., 19. In an *Atlantic* article of his own, Bascom criticized the elective as too isolating and indiscriminate to serve the public good. As he put it, "remote lines of inquiry . . . arrest [the] fellowship of thought." He goes on to say that if "we must have superficiality, let it be the superficiality associated with wide surfaces, not that of minute knowledge." John Bascom, "Changes in College Life, *The Atlantic* 91 (1903): 752; 757.

70. Curti, *The University of Wisconsin*, 284.

71. John Bascom, "A Christian State," Address given at the University of Wisconsin, June 19, 1887 (Milwaukee, WI: Cramer, Aikens and Cramer, 1887), 6; Something like the course elective, driven by specialized interest, would endanger the perfect balance Bascom sought between individual and social good. He explains this balance at one point in terms of intensity and generality: Intensity is not allowed to gain ground at the expense of generality, or generality at the cost of intensity." Ibid., 9.

72. Ibid., 28.

73. Ibid.

74. Ibid., 30.

75. Hoeveler, "The University and the Social Gospel," 298. The vision crystalized under the administration of Charles R. Van Hise, president of the University of Wisconsin after 1902. Van Hise transformed Bascom's "sense of spiritual power into a doctrine of economic growth. This dogma [that] defined the state university's research activity, for new knowledge must be applied directly to the improvement of the lives of the people . . . virtually every home or business in the state, from machine shops to model dairy farms, would feel the long outreach of the state university."

76. Vannevar Bush. *Science: The Endless Frontier* (Washington, DC: United States Government Printing Office, 1945).

77. Bush. *Science*, 15.

78. Ibid., 9.

79. Scott J. Peters, Theodore R. Alter, and Neil Schartzbach, *Democracy and Higher Education: Traditions and Stories of Civic Engagement* (East Lansing: Michigan State University Press, 2010).

80. Friedrich Kittler, "Universities: Wet, Hard, Soft, and Harder," *Critical Inquiry* 31, no. 1 (2004): 244–255.

81. Daniel C. Gilman, "The Building of the University," An Inaugural Address Delivered at Oakland November 7, 1872 (San Francisco: John H. Carmany & Co. Book and Job Printers), 5.

82. Daniel C. Gilman, "The Benefits Which Society Derives from Universities," *Nature 33*, no. 847 (1886): 6.

83. Ibid., 7.

84. W. Carson Ryan, *Studies in Early Graduate Education: The John Hopkins, Clark University, University of Chicago* (Boston, MA: Merrymount Press, 1939), 55.

85. G. Stanley Hall, "Third Annual Report of the President to the Board of Trustees," (Worchester, MA: April 1893), 14. Box 77, Presidential Reports. Archives and Special Collections, Clark University, Worchester, MA.

86. Ryan, *Studies in Early Graduate*, 80. Even its graduate program was spare. The university conferred 257 doctorates in its first thirty years.

87. G. Stanley Hall, "Clark University," *Science* ns-15.362 (January 10, 1890): 8.

88. Ibid.

89. Ibid. Hall repeated this argument in his second annual report to the trustees: "No university is strong enough to work all of the vast and ever widening frontiers of human knowledge." G. Stanley Hall, "Second Annual Report of the President to the Board of Trustees," (Worchester, MA: September 29, 1891): 6.

90. Hall, "Clark University," 18.

91. G.S. Hall, "First Annual Report of the President to the Board of Trustees," (Worchester, MA: October 4, 1890): 11; G.S. Hall, Editorial. *Pedagogical Seminary* 1, no. 1 (1891a): 121.

92. Hall, "First Annual Report," 52.

93. Ibid., 19–20.

94. Ibid., 24.

95. Ibid., 52.

96. Paul D. Travers, "G. Stanley Hall: Pioneer in Comparative Education," *The Educational Forum* 33, no. 3 (1969): 301–305; Lester F. Goodchild, "G. Stanley Hall and the Study of Higher Education," *The Review of Higher Education* 20, no. 1 (1996): 69–99. The pioneering program was the first to offer comparative study of higher education. Its curriculum included history, facilities management, finance and research funding, teacher training, associations, curricula, institutional missions, and public policy.

97. G. Stanley Hall, Editorial. *Pedagogical Seminary* 1, no. 1 (1891a): 121; 122. As Hall puts it, "Strength lies in individualization." The problem, he goes on to say, is "falsely understood 'general culture.'"

98. G. Stanley Hall, Editorial. *Pedagogical Seminary 1*, no.3 (1891c): 323.

99. G. Stanley Hall, "Contemporary University Problems," *The Pedagogical Seminary* 21, no. 2 (1914): 248.

100. Ibid., 252.

101. Hall, Editorial. *Pedagogical Seminary 1*, no.3 (1891c): 323.

102. The history of California's master plan that I detail in chapter 4 illustrates this attitudinal shift.

103. William Chance, "A Vision in Progress: The Decision to Establish a Public University at Monterey Bay, An Occasional Paper" (San Jose, CA: California Higher Education Policy Center, 1997).

104. Donald R. Gerth, *The People's University: A History of the California State University* (CA: Berkeley Public Policy Press, 2010), 566. Leon Panetta, then a congressman, played a key role in securing federal funding for the new campus.

105. Chance, "A Vision in Progress."

106. Ibid.

107. "A Vision for Learning: Transforming the Paradigm for Higher Education in the 21st Century," (Seaside, CA: 1997): 5. [CSUMB Self-Study]

108. John Vasconcellos, and the Joint Committee for Review of the Master Plan for Higher Education, "California faces . . . California's Future: Education for Citizenship in a Multicultural Democracy," (Sacramento: California State Assembly, 1989).

109. "A Vision for Learning," 396.

110. California's master plan concentrated inquiry at UC campuses. The CSUs were given a teaching mission. What encouragement there was for regional research positioned it as limited in relevance and value.

111. "CSU Office of the Chancellor News Release," (March 17, 1993): Manuscript No. 1, Box 7, Series 8, Misc Subjects, File #9, Fort Ord Campus Initiative, 1993–1994. Armando Arias Archive. Tanimura & Antle Family Memorial Library Archives and Special Collectives, California State University Monterey Bay, Seaside, CA. A 1993 press release from the CSU Office of the Chancellor announcing Steven Arvizu as interim provost of CSUMB describes CSUMB as "a multiuniversity redevelopment effort which includes a joint CSU/UC educational and research center."

112. "California State University, Monterey Bay, Vision Statement" (Seaside, CA: September 27, 1994).

113. Marsha Moroh (Dean of the School of Science, Media Arts and Technology) in conversation with the author (Seaside, CA: March 13, 2013).

114. Ibid.

115. "1st Progress Report, Watershed Ecology Outreach Program," (Moss Landing Marine Laboratories, Benthic Lab, September 1994). Manuscript No. 1, Box 2, Series 1, Academic Programs and Policies, File #77, Watershed Project, 1994–1995. Armando Arias Archive. Tanimura & Antle Family Memorial Library Archives and Special Collections, California State University Monterey Bay, Seaside, CA.

116. "Center for Arts, Human Communication, and Creative Technologies Academic Philosophy and Programs," (August 2, 1995): 9; Manuscript No. 1, Box 1, Series 1—Academic Programs and Policies, File #20—Centers & Institutions, 1995—1996. Armando Arias Archive. Tanimura & Antle Family Memorial Library Archives and Special Collections, California State University Monterey Bay, Seaside, CA.

117. Ibid., 10–11.

118. Eliot and his argument about the importance of maturity in students might have contributed to this belief.

119. Seth Pollack (Director, CSUMB Service Learning Institute) in conversation with the author (Seaside, CA: October 13, 2014).

120. "A Vision for Learning," 195.

121. Pollack.

122. "A Vision for Learning," 195.

123. "A Vision for Learning," 206.

124. Pollack.

125. Ibid.

126. Ibid.

127. Ibid.

128. Pollack spoke to this connection when talking about his experience at Stanford after the Peace Corp. He described Stanford as "a wonderful place. . . . Yet, their place in the world is to develop new knowledge and to own that process, and to name it, and to give it titles and create its lineage. There's a conflict there within acknowledging that there's other knowledge structures out there that might also be valid and important, and even relevant and maybe, just maybe, even more relevant in some contexts than others."

129. Ibid.

130. Member of the Evergreen faculty in conversation with the author (Olympia, WA, October 21, 2013).

131. Paul Westmeyer, *An Analytic History of American Higher Education* (Springfield, IL: Charles C. Thomas, 1997), 69.

132. Member of the Evergreen faculty in conversation with the author (Olympia, WA, October 21, 2013).

133. Ibid.

134. Barbara Smith (Evergreen's Vice President for Academic Affairs and Provost from 1994 to 2001) in conversation with the author (San Jose, CA, Oct 12, 2012).

135. For a period of time, Evergreen faculty offered upper-division classes at Grays Harbor College an hour outside Olympia.

136. Member of the Evergreen faculty in conversation with the author (Olympia, WA, October 21, 2013).

137. Zoltan Grossman (Evergreen faculty) in conversation with the author (Olympia, WA, October 22, 2013).

138. Ibid.

139. Ibid.

Chapter Four

Losing Sight of Invention

Evergreen and CSUMB joined an American tradition of experimentation in higher education when they embraced alternative educational practices. Unlike their predecessors, they were bound by legislative and professional infrastructure that did not exist in the nineteenth and early twentieth centuries. Each had to navigate the national and state educational policies that now govern academic institutions. The two hoped to distinguish their campuses from more established schools by avoiding some of higher education's bureaucracy. In a 1970 progress report on campus planning, Dean E. Clabaugh, Evergreen's Vice President for Business, presented Evergreen as an opportunity to design a school without legislative dictates.[1] Unlike California, Washington had no master plan for higher education, a lack that Clabaugh characterized as "tremendously advantageous, because it precludes the 'stamping out' of another institution with the same approach as those existing, however excellent they may be."[2] Clabaugh cites Washington governor Daniel J. Evans's remarks about the calcification of academic institutions and the need for a "flexible and sophisticated educational instrument" that could "'unshackle our educational thinking from traditional patterns'."[3] The founding faculty at CSUMB expressed a similar desire to avoid "stamping out" another institution. As the Vice President of Academic Affairs, Armando Arias put it in CSUMB's 1997 self-study, the university hoped to "'avoid paralyzing bureaucracy and create enabling infrastructure'."[4]

Evergreen and CSUMB embraced an anti-bureaucratic ethos as part of their nontraditional image. In practice, they still had to earn accreditation, follow federal and state financial aid guidelines, adhere to fire codes, and work cooperatively with other campuses. They had to do so, not because higher education is mired in needless bureaucracy, but because education necessitates institutional constraints. The institutional designs that pepper

American higher education are the result of colleges and universities search-ing for different ways to organize themselves. Administrative mechanisms are often the only visible manifestations of those efforts, which can fuel the impression that colleges and universities hinder access to educational content more than they facilitate it. When the administration is visible but the educa-tional reasons for it are not, critics find fault with what they can see: institu-tions that appear driven by bureaucracy.

In CSUMB's case, critics faulted the nascent institution for failing to deliver on its promise of an alternative curriculum. CSUMB did not realize all its goals, but it did find novel ways of satisfying California's transfer policies while challenging the tradition of differentiated function. From the outset, CSUMB recognized the role that credit transfer played in its vision of serving the region's migrant and Latinx populations.[5] At the time of its 1997 self-study, 60 percent of CSUMB students were transfers. It would have been shortsighted of CSUMB to design a curriculum without regard for students seeking to transfer. As Shenk explained, everything about CSUMB's early years, "was about articulation."[6] The campus had a vision, Shenk explained, but it lacked the "ability to put into place the structures or the systems, the administrative systems" needed to realize it.[7] CSUMB's 1997 Self-Study explained the dilemma the campus faced. Its university learning require-ments:

> constitute a type of academic currency which differs from the course and credit currency used in most institutions of higher education. And, difficulties in converting from one system to another have posed serious challenges to CSUMB's efforts to accommodate the needs of students seeking to transfer into and out of this university. This same issue has complicated efforts to establish inter-institutional curricular articulation agreements, most notably with CSUMB's primary feeder community colleges.[8]

California law constrained CSUMB's curricular choices.[9] It would not have been possible, for instance, for CSUMB to offer something akin to Ever-green's "upside down degree," which allows students enrolled in its reserva-tion programs to begin with their specialization and finish with general studies.

This chapter contextualizes CSUMB's efforts to realize an unconvention-al curriculum within the history of credit transfer, the Donahoe Higher Edu-cation Act known as the California Master Plan for Higher Education, and the notion of differentiation of function. Considered within the context of that history and policy, the labyrinthine bureaucracy of credit transfer initial-ly seems the greatest barrier to the new university with CSUMB's unusual design only adding layers of administrative complexity. However, credit transfer cannot be understood apart from differentiated functions and the structuring role they played in the California's master plan. Prior to adoption of that unifying plan, inventive educational ideas emerged at each of the state's campuses. Each had its own institutional arrangements and reasons for it. The master plan's notion of differentiation of function suppressed many of those efforts. Credit transfer was the administrative mechanism that enabled coordination between three systems with differentiated functions. Transfer policies restrict independent program and curriculum development within the individual campuses that comprise California's tiered system. The University of California (UC), for instance, can justify its monopoly over inquiry on the grounds that students can transfer between schools to access that aspect of the academic project.

In effect, the combination of differentiated functions and credit transfer polices—the very policies that stymied CSUMB's curricular plans—serve to restrict higher education's critical modalities by obscuring differences between campuses. Credit transfer in particular makes it harder to see variations between campuses and the localized work that shapes educational arrangements.

The following history of credit transfer shows how California has used it to flatten and smooth education. However, CSUMB's story suggests that credit transfer need not discourage critique or the invention it fosters. It need not be restrictive. It could amplify institutional differences while still facilitating student movement. It could do so by minimizing differentiation of function and placing greater value on the features that distinguish one school from another. Such an approach would change the optics on higher education by once again making educational choices visible.

Transfer Agreements

The administrative instruments that govern credit transfers, known either as transfer or articulation agreements, thread the needle between "enabling infrastructure" and "paralyzing bureaucracy." Their stated purpose is to ease the bureaucratic obstacles that otherwise deter students from pursuing a degree. Many students would not continue their studies without mechanisms in place that guarantee the transfer of completed course work. Transfer agreements facilitate movement between schools by reducing administrative obstacles. As one advocate described it, transfer is "a procedure that should provide a continuous, smooth flow of students from grade to grade and school to school."[10] While the purpose of a transfer agreement is to simplify enrollment management, the agreement itself is a complex administrative instrument. Mandated by state legislatures, governed by system-wide policies, and administered on a case-by-case basis, they can epitomize educational bureaucracy. To achieve harmonious flow, colleges and universities agree to accept credits that students have completed at other institutions. The *California Articulation Policies and Procedures Handbook* explains the basis for those agreements, underscoring that "courses are not to be construed as 'equivalent' but rather as comparable, or acceptable in lieu of each other."[11] Drafting and maintaining agreements thus requires its own infrastructure. Schools establish transfer agreements on a course-by-course basis to ensure that content is comparable. That process is time and labor intensive. Arthur M. Cohen describes credit transfer as "a swirling relationship based on student situational characteristics rather than a linear process in which attendance follows a pattern of lower-division completion at one institution followed by matriculation and subsequent baccalaureate receipt at another."[12] The practice of credit transfer must be responsive to the local details of the student seeking transfer. Multiply those individual details by thousands—a 2012 National Student Clearinghouse Research Center study found that one-third of all students change institutions before earning a degree—and the complexities of administering transfer become clear.[13] A 1955 report on California higher education explained the "complicated problems" behind those numbers including the need to establish a means of assessing earned credits and the "difficult and important problems of counseling and guidance."[14] A 2010 report on transfer and articulation in California described a process mired in complexities even with the assistance of statewide planning tools and oversight committees.[15]

The credit transfer infrastructure that exists today is the result of decades of experiments in enrollment policies and curricular design. Daniel Gilman first modified the bachelor's degree at Johns Hopkins University so that Baltimore youth could obtain a degree in two years.[16] While president of the University of Chicago, William Rainey Harper, addressed what he called student "migration" by distinguishing lower from upper-division classes and assigning responsibility for the former to what he called the "junior colleges."[17] As the idea of upper and lower divisions gained support, additional distinctions were made between lower-division courses in technical and applied arts and courses in civics, liberal arts, and science.[18] David Starr Jordan, president of the Leland Stanford Junior University, lobbied to eliminate the upper division at smaller colleges and the lower-division or "elementary" courses at the universities.[19] At the same time, the University of California, Berkeley "created a wall between the upper and lower divisions" and Alexis F. Lange, a dean at Berkeley, undertook an effort to require California's junior colleges to replicate the lower-division curriculum offered at the UC.[20] Colleges and universities experimented with variations on this idea for decades.[21] These administrative experiments influenced the first rudimentary transfer agreements and gradually fueled the growth of the community colleges, which more than doubled in number between 1966 and 1982 from 565 to 1,219.[22] They are the predecessors to what is now a commonplace practice in which colleges and universities treat an associate's degree as comparable to the lower-division requirements at a four-year institution.[23]

The administrative details of credit transfer are sufficiently complex that national committees began to form in the 1950s to create guidelines for transferring from junior to senior institutions.[24] All fifty states had a coordinating authority by the 1990s and Richard S. Mosholder and Christopher J. Zirkle explain that, "most were actively promoting integrated programs, each of which was essentially unique."[25] Some of those guidelines aimed at mitigating prejudices against students transferring from a community college to a four-year institution.[26] In many cases, state legislatures initiated the transfer effort and directed state councils and committees to negotiate agreements; state oversight guarded against "inflexible and arbitrary" transfer plans.[27] The evolution of credit transfer in California followed national trends. At midcentury, California had established a University-Junior-College Conference Committee on Relations charged with reviewing architecture, business administration, engineering, and home economics programs while another committee oversaw guidance counseling related to credit transfer.[28] In the 1970s, California charged the California Postsecondary Education Commission with ensuring efficient use of state funds and the elimination of unnecessary duplication. To further coordinate between systems and campuses, the California Intersegmental Articulation Council, a professional organization for articulation personnel, convened in the 1990s and launched a newsletter, *The Articulated Voice*.

Individual campuses also built what a 1955 report described as, "extensive liaison machinery" to support transfer agreements.[29] That machinery took different forms depending on the basis for credit transfer, itself a contentious question. In the first national study of transfer students, Dorothy M. Knoell and Leland L. Medsker (1965) expressed concern that discrepancies in grading procedures overestimated student readiness and recommended testing for aptitude rather than accepting credits as a sign of achievement. Later studies recommended the "[c]areful development of catalog course descriptions" so that they might serve as the basis for decisions about course equivalencies.[30] In the 1980s, California adopted a common course numbering system called the California Articulation Number to further facilitate credit transfer.

Even with workable transfer agreements in place, schools found that the process was not self-evident to students, nor was the practice as simple as moving earned credits from one institution to another. Those credits represent specific educational experiences that do not transfer as easily as the credits. As they recognized the complexities of the process, schools developed advising services to help students make the transition from general education to coursework in the major.[31] The need for transfer-related advising and a growing recognition of the role that community colleges played in serving women, minorities, and other historically underserved populations led California to pilot twenty transfer centers in the 1980s aimed at increasing transfer rates. [32] In the present day, transfer offices are a standard feature on every campus. California colleges and universities regularly update their curriculums in an online database called the ASSIST Coordination Site and California's Intersegmental Major Preparation Articulated Curriculum brings together faculty and staff from the community colleges, the CSU, and the UC to coordinate curricular design and ensure that lower-division courses adequately prepare students for upper-division work in the major.

The universal adoption of the Carnegie Unit may be the single biggest factor in the eventual success of transfer agreements. The unit functions as a currency capable of resolving all manner of discrepancies in instruction and content between institutions. The Carnegie Foundation for the Advancement of Teaching established the Carnegie Unit in the early twentieth century as the basis for a teacher pension system. The instrument continues to govern scheduling, graduation requirements, faculty workloads, and financial aid eligibility. A 2015 Carnegie Foundation report described it as the "common language to organize the work of schooling and communicate student accomplishments across a wide range of institutions."[33] It enables unconventional schools like Evergreen and CSUMB to articulate their programs with more conventional academic systems. It makes it possible for Evergreen to use grade-less, narrative-based transcripts without jeopardizing students' ability to transfer their work to another school. The Carnegie Unit helped educators to embrace the idea that course work earned at another college or university was comparable to their own. Once those comparisons seemed plausible, colleges and universities then pursued institutional congruence by adopting similar content and learning objectives, especially in the lower division. [34]

Even though transfer agreements treat credits as "comparable" rather than "equivalent," transfer processes foster the impression that educational programs are interchangeable and thus education independent of its institutional form. By design, transfer agreements obscure the circumstances and details that distinguish one campus, curriculum, or course from another. When four-year colleges and universities exercise oversight of associate's degrees so they can be "assured" of "a universally acceptable level of quality," they must gloss the material and professional differences between schools that they would otherwise tout as evidence of their distinctive offerings. [35] Schools honor credits earned at other intuitions by highlighting points of commonality and suppressing differences. Organizational variances disappear. The ways in which credit transfer appears to separate educational content from a specific campus generates the impression that the unusual features that schools cultivate have little bearing on the education they supply.

Reconciling Accessible with Distinct in California

The history of California's master plan for higher education is a study in the ways that transfer agreements, in the name of accessibility, obscure and dull the distinctive offerings of each individual campus. California eventually achieved its goal of articulating its colleges and universities, but that articulation came at the expense of the local and regional differences that shaped each school. One of the ways that CSUMB challenged the educational status quo was by refusing the role assigned to it in California's tiered model of differentiated function. In doing so, the university made visible the historical decisions behind the plan and opened up possibilities for alternative ways of conceptualizing and organizing education.

Adopted in 1960 during "a chaotic and unstructured time in California's development of . . . higher education," the Donahoe Higher Education Act formally recognized three systems: the University of California, the California State University, and the community colleges.[36] The plan assigns each a different mission and structure. Those differentiated functions remain visible today in a range of policies and practices including enrollment management. Under current California law, the UC guarantees admittance to the top 9 percent of students in each graduating high school class; the CSU gives preference in admission to students from the service area of each campus, and the community colleges maintain open enrollment policies.

A 1989 report by the California State Assembly identified student transfer as the main idea behind the Master Plan: "Transfer is the promise at the center of California's entire system of higher education. The idea is deceptively simple. Wherever you start, whatever your past scores and grades, no matter whether you bring a history of 'achievement' or the promise of your initiative and commitment: we will provide an opportunity for you."[37] In addition to outlining the missions and domains of each system, the plan mandates that the three cooperate in making higher education accessible to Californians. It took decades of additional work and legislation to achieve the goal of articulating the state's community colleges to the CSU and the UC. California adopted a number of mechanisms to achieve its goal including a "unified" core curriculum that would transfer between its three systems, a common course numbering system, and "carefully articulated lower- and upper-division courses across majors."[38] The state legislature passed the California Student Transfer Achievement Reform Act in 2010, fifty years after the Master Plan. The UC finalized transfer pathways in 2015.[39]

The slow pace of policy change is due in large part to the enduring interest in maintaining three systems with three different missions. In the debates that shaped the Master Plan, educators argued over whom should have access to the liberal arts and how best to organize academic inquiry. The decisions they made continue to shape California's current enrollment and transfer policies. The result is a tiered educational system premised on merit that treats credit hours as interchangeable while preventing the three systems from acting interchangeably. The credit hours are interchangeable, but institutional mission, average course sizes, average teaching load, budgets, hiring and retention policies, and resources and holdings are not. These structural differences have prevented the CSUs and community colleges from more fully exploring institutional possibilities when they emerge.

Before California Had a Master Plan

Regionalism played a prominent role in the early development of California higher education. From the last part of the nineteenth century until the state adopted its master plan in 1960, California was home to a collection of normal schools, public regional colleges, junior colleges, and UC campuses. Where other states took a global perspective to institutional growth and, as in the case of the University of Wisconsin, imagined the state university extending all the way to the state borders, California organized higher education in a piecemeal fashion. It founded distinct campuses with distinct missions, region by region.

As California founded normal schools and UC campuses, each one acquired local features and rhythms that educators only later (and begrudgingly) changed or revised in the effort to coordinate with other campuses. Only after the state had established three normal schools in San Jose, Los Angeles, and Chico, for instance, did the three adopt a common academic calendar.[40] The UC system at the time consisted of the Berkeley campus and its satellites: the California State Normal School in Los Angeles, an oceanography laboratory in San Diego, a farm in Davis, and the Citrus Experiment Station in Riverside. The satellite campuses both expanded the UC offerings and continued to reflect local influence. Unlike the UCs, each state college was sovereign and they did not become a system until designated one in California's master plan.

Some of the same objectives that drive higher education today are visible in that earlier landscape. The state developed its flagship university, for instance, to fuel economic growth and it established satellite campuses as a way to organize research into different areas of study. The state founded regional teaching colleges, likewise, to meet the need for qualified professionals. Other factors that influenced the early development of higher education reflect the thinking of that time. Trade schools, junior colleges, teaching colleges, and agricultural programs, for instance, were born of the belief that students need only aspire to the level of education suited to their social position. As the Carnegie Commission put it in its 1932 report on California: "each kind of schooling provided will enlist the students best fitted to receive it."[41] Social prejudices fueled the belief that each school should tailor their course offerings to their distinct student population, be it women, immigrants, or the working class.

Motivated by external pressures and internal missions, California campuses grew and diversified. The normal schools became teaching colleges, some of which hosted junior colleges, and the UC satellites developed into universities in their own right. Along the way, the pressure to increase the number of people pursuing a college degree tangled with the belief that many students, including women and minorities, lacked the intellectual capacity needed to undertake scientific and philosophical inquiries and other advanced studies. Before the state fully embraced the idea of transfer, a seismic shift had to occur in beliefs about higher education's purpose and its place in the lives of all students.

Differentiation of Function

As individual campuses developed, redundancies in course offerings, programs, majors, and degrees began to occur. The debate over whether and how to assign differentiated functions to California's colleges and universities started with the question of whether founding an agricultural institute at California State Polytechnic College would detract from the UC's efforts to establish a farm in Davis.[42] The question of Cal Poly involved two factors—institutional mission and geography—that would vex educators and legislators for years as they worked to articulate the state's colleges and universities. The question was bound on the one side by the UC's exclusive claim to research and the belief that inquiry should be restricted to the state's designated research university. It was bound on the other by the interests of the state's leading industries, the regional differences between farms, and the potential benefits of establishing agricultural research programs in different parts of the state. The decision came down to whether or not to honor the differentiated missions of the schools involved, or leverage regional differences in such a way that might better serve industry, another mission of California higher education.[43]

An exception was made in the case of Cal Poly in the name of balance, but balance proved harder to achieve when the curriculum under question was the liberal arts rather than agriculture. A debate began in the 1920s over whether or not California's teacher colleges should be allowed to open their upper-division courses to subjects beyond teacher training and offer the liberal arts. When the teaching colleges first proposed broadening their mission, they faced criticism from the UC for "aspiring to become regional colleges offering courses of study parallel to those of the university."[44] A 1932 report on California higher education commissioned by the legislature and conducted by the Carnegie Foundation for the Advancement of Teaching found in favor of the UC and characterized the state college programs as *"pseudo-senior colleges"* lacking in legal basis. [45]

Throughout the 1932 report, the Carnegie Foundation argues the importance of cultivating institutional diversity among California's campuses. It argues just as strenuously for greater articulation. The Foundation characterized California public higher education as having benefited from "a period of extensive experimentation" but suffering a "problem of policy and organization" born of "a notable lack of unity" in its administration. [46] The report exacerbated tensions without offering resolution. Their conflicting advice proved influential on subsequent studies and laid the groundwork for a master plan that attempted to balance distinct with accessible.

The commission made its most forceful case for diversification in their concluding remarks about the junior and state colleges. The junior colleges, the report cautions, should not suppose their "inferior status," or always look "upward to the university to discover its functions, its point of view, its procedures, and its social philosophy." [47] When the junior colleges act as "mere university preparatory schools," they forfeit their role as "the highest part of community education for a general civilized life." [48] The report urges junior college teachers to show greater discretion and it discourages the "slavish" imitation of university lower-division courses then encouraged by UC Berkeley. [49] The authors have similar advice for the state colleges, which they urge not to organize by "one pattern of function or organization." [50] They should instead individualize, a practice that has "greatly dulled of late by the recent tendency of every higher institution to do what every other does." [51]

The authors of the 1932 report were just as adamant that California higher education needed better articulation. The report faults both a "lack of articulation among the various units of the educational system" and "regional rivalries and local ambitions" for generating the "controversies over admission requirements, transfer regulations, and curricula." [52] The authors find little to commend about existing administration, characterizing it as "the accidental product" of local political pressure. [53] They are emphatic about the solution: "Coordination, not reconstruction, is the need." [54] California, they argue, will not attain the social benefits of education nor meet its obligations if it does not address the "lack of the necessary machinery to make effective the coordination of the several phases of higher education." [55] They recommend greater unity and integration as remedies. In a third line of argument, the report reprimands schools for failing to clarify the differences between the colleges and the universities and encouraging too many students to pursue university preparation through the study of liberal subjects. [56] Universal access to a university degree, the authors argue, was never the intent. "A university's first obligation," they clarify, "is to select and educate those who give promise of being the ethical and scholarly leaders in their professions."[57] By setting educational standards, colleges and universities protect "that portion of society that has the good sense to be discriminating."[58]

The 1932 Carnegie report is unequivocal in its call for greater articulation between the community colleges, state colleges, and the UC. It is equally adamant that California's colleges and universities were not equivalent. The authors underscore that each institution serves different student populations and should tailor their work to their distinct missions. The report envisions higher education operating as a sophisticated sorting machine that efficiently directs students toward the programs best suited to their interests and abilities while also "finding and encouraging submerged talents."[59]

The desire to differentiate the colleges from the universities while safeguarding accessibility persisted into the next phase of California higher education, but the desire among the state colleges to chart their own course proved just as strong. Their transformation continued despite the Carnegie report. Donald R. Gerth suggests that the strong regional identification of each college and the fact that "legislators clearly regarded their [district] campuses as their own" led the colleges to forge ahead with new programs against the recommendations of the 1932 report.[60] In 1935, the state allowed the teachers colleges to drop the word "teachers" from their names and offer liberal arts degrees.

Finding Answers in the Administrative Weeds

The effort on the part of the colleges to diversify themselves met with backlash from the UC. Under the leadership of Robert Sproul, UC president from 1928 to 1958, and Clark Kerr, UC president from 1958 to 1967, the University of California lobbied for a tiered system of higher education that clearly differentiated the university from the colleges. The campaign intensified when the state colleges petitioned to offer engineering degrees, a development that Sproul opposed.[61] In the hope of restricting the scope and mission of the colleges to teacher credentialing, the UC regents, the California State Board of Education, and the State Assembly appointed the Strayer committee to determine how the state could best organize higher education. The committee issued its recommendations in 1948 and those along with the findings of a restudy published in 1955 formed the basis for the master plan adopted by the State Assembly in 1960.

The Strayer committee tackled the question of how best to organize the various aspects and domains of higher education by digging into administrative detail. They appreciated "the need for flexibility," and, as they put it, "to make the school serve the needs of the student rather than the student fit the pattern of the school."[62] In the following representative excerpt, for instance, they describe the instructional relevance of classroom and course scheduling. Design elements such as course sequencing, they suggest, not only assist with learning but also shape the contours of areas of study by ensuring that certain kinds of information and training relate.

> Many courses must be presented in carefully determined sequences; many must be integrated with laboratory courses to be pursued concurrently; many must be so scheduled as to avoid conflict with other courses in the same field, or in related fields, in order to insure that continuity of experiences necessary for the understanding and appreciation of the major problems in each field of interest. [63]

They again focus on administrative detail when addressing the question of how best to distribute instruction and inquiry responsibilities among California's colleges and universities. In the years following the 1932 Carnegie report, the state colleges had found the domain of teacher education elastic enough to encompass most subjects. Over the years they had stretched that domain to expand their curricular offerings and meet the needs of local students, many of whom would not leave their home region to attend a university and not all of whom wished to become teachers. While their expanded domain arguably aligned with their mission, the Strayer committee (like the Carnegie committee before it) felt the state colleges encroached on the UC's domain. "The state colleges," they underscore, "are not responsible for graduate work involving research, nor for education for the professions with the exception of teaching." [64] Moreover, they argue, the UC could only devote itself "freely and continuously to the slow processes of scholarship, research, and the extension of the frontiers of knowledge" so long as California "made other provision for taking care of large numbers of students who need education beyond high school." [65] It should be ensured, they conclude, that state funding for academic research "not be dissipated among several institutions." [66]

Unlike the Carnegie committee, the Strayer committee did not attempt to justify restrictions on the state colleges by citing the needs of different student populations. Instead, they addressed the question of domains as a practical matter akin to course sequencing. The organizational challenge of accommodating a growing student population without diminishing the university's other functions, they argued, necessitated a systematic division of the different stages of education and academic responsibilities. The Strayer report thus settled the question of differentiated function and raised a host of other questions about where and how to organize and maintain each aspect and domain of higher education.

Following the recommendations of the Strayer report, the California Master Plan organized higher education into a neat division of labor. The lines of demarcation are clear. The community and the state colleges are responsible for the bulk of lower- and upper-division undergraduate instruction. The UC dedicates its infrastructure primarily to inquiry and scholarship; the UC produces knowledge; the other colleges and universities disseminate it. When the drafting of a master plan for California higher education began, a majority of the thirteen state colleges, all still independent of one another, objected to any division of labor that prevented them from offering doctorates or that hindered their ability to develop research programs.[67] Nevertheless, the draft that became law positioned the state colleges as the Strayer committee imagined them: somewhere "beyond the technical level of the junior college and below the professional schools of the University."[68] It allowed the state colleges to pursue research related to instruction and to offer joint doctorates with the UC; it did not make provisions for open-ended research or independent doctorates at the state colleges.[69] It also reorganized the colleges into a system. The thirteen campuses, which at the time ranged from three to one hundred years in age, faced the question of how to coordinate with each other while maintaining the differentiated functions outlined in the Master Plan.

Making Inquiry's Infrastructure Invisible

Before the state adopted a master plan, California's community and state colleges designed curriculum to meet the needs of the students in their service areas including students who wished to attend the nearest campus but did not want a career in teaching. Those needs included transferrable credit hours, which schools met with liberal arts programs and other preparation for advanced studies. The colleges expanded their offerings when faculty decided that all students would benefit from exposure to the liberal arts. The 1955 follow up to the Strayer report applauded the curricular experimentation at the state colleges.[70] The report found the colleges has benefited from "the absence of typical academic traditions," and had "experimented in the field of general education" which had "maintained virility and flexibility in the college programs."[71] The authors also applauded institutional diversity among the colleges: "While there is much in common among the colleges, they are not similar enough to be considered as a group of institutions with a single purpose, nor can they always be administered by uniform procedures."[72] They had achieved that diversity, the report notes, "under some difficulty, being bound by State laws and regulations designed largely for other kinds of State institutions more uniformly regulated and with more uniform service than that performed by a college."[73]

In the wake of the Master Plan, the community colleges and the state universities continued to design curricula to meet students' needs, but faced tighter restrictions and more levels of administration including oversight by the State Department of Finance and the Coordinating Council for Higher Education.[74] Under the terms of the Master Plan, they could not develop the kinds of advanced degrees that enable a school to support research programs. The Master Plan itself became justification for allowing or denying the col-

leges to pursue various programs. As the 1955 restudy explained with re-
gards to a proposed enology program at Fresno State, for instance, the cost of
training specialists was high enough that it could only be justified by maintaining differentiated functions between the systems as outlined in the Master
Plan. The study explained the economics of differentiated function like so:
"the cost of preparing the small number of specialists in enology graduated at
the Davis campus of the University would not be justified were it not inci-
dental to research in this important aspect of the State's agricultural economy."[75] The same logic did not extend, however, to an "occupational"
program at Fresno State, which "would not be a justifiable claim upon the
State, since the number of graduates required by the industry in any one year
would be relatively small and the expenditure for educating them large."[76]

The colleges nevertheless continued to experiment with their offerings
including seeking research opportunities in areas like business, public administration, agriculture, and applied arts. Some of the programs contributed to
or helped to define new professional fields, such as offering training in living
assistance for people with disabilities.

A discussion among presidents of state colleges hosted by Boise State
College in 1968–1969 suggests that regionalism continued to serve as a
productive design constraint on institutional planning. A comment by Robert
Johns, president of Sacramento State College, illustrates: "Might not this
institution, because of the nature of its location, do something with its legal
definition that may not be done if it were located, say in Wallace, or Priest
Lake or somewhere else?"[77] A 1970s inventory of agricultural programs
commissioned by the state gives a sense of how colleges carved out specialized areas of study in response to local circumstances and statewide coordination efforts. California hosted a total of forty-four agricultural programs at
that time—thirty-seven at the community colleges, four at the state colleges,
and three at the UC.[78] The demand for agricultural studies exceeded the
available offerings, but the expense of farmland, livestock, and sophisticated
equipment made it cost prohibitive to have programs on every campus. In his
recommendations to the California State Coordinating Council for Higher
Education, the report's author, George A. Gries, urged campuses to expand
existing programs, share resources, and facilitate credit transfer. "Great improvement could come about," he concluded, with "more harmonious interaction between the institutions."[79] Programs could accommodate need, he
suggested, by occasionally "swapping" faculty rather than transferring students.[80] The California State Colleges also floated the possibility of a joint
veterinary program with the UC that would make use of existing livestock
facilities at Cal Poly and Cal Poly Pomona.[81] The UC opted instead for
expanding the veterinary program at Davis to ensure it would be "the highest
possible quality."[82] As evidenced by the UC's decision, the investment in
differentiated function generally discouraged the kind of cross-institutional

collaboration that Gries advocated. With other avenues to program growth closed to them, the state universities continued to tailor their offerings to local need and experiment with specialization. Those efforts led to programs in animal science at California State University, Chico, plant science at California State University, Fresno, and ornamental horticulture at Cal Poly Ponoma.[83] One program offered a course in Spanish for agricultural workers.[84]

Citing differentiated function, California prevented its community colleges and state universities from developing specialized offerings. The colleges circumvented those restrictions as best they could by developing practical and "applied" offerings such as training aids to assist people with disabilities or programs in police work.[85] State policies, however, prevented them from developing those offerings into the kind of expansive and exploratory areas of inquiry that today go by the name of disability studies and justice studies.

From the state's perspective, it was unfeasible to fund libraries, laboratories, graduate programs, and a full slate of departments at every campus. Likewise, it discouraged the colleges from pursuing research without those resources and without an organizational structure in which research could benefit from the close proximity of diverse fields. Such were the state's reasons for a model of higher education that "concentrated" research "in a few centers."[86]

In practice, instruction and inquiry took place to greater and lesser degrees throughout California's complex educational landscape. It was difficult to see that work, however, due to the differentiated functions assigned to the three different systems and the division of curriculum into upper and lower sections. Even advocates of differentiated function struggled with where to draw the line between instruction and inquiry and settled for inexact rules of thumb, such as distinguishing between California-specific research and specialized research of global interest.[87] A 1989 legislative report, for instance, drew geographical boundaries around research domains: "we support research undertaken at the California State University when it studies an issue or problem relevant to the changing social, environmental, economic, or cultural life of any of California's many regions."[88]

The debates over differentiated function persisted when schools found that scaffolding up education by assigning campuses different "levels" did not settle the question of how research related to teaching, or how best to organize inquiry. Through a complex arrangement of admissions policies and course sequencing designed to manage workload, California's tiered system succeeded primarily in determining which students would have access to research opportunities and which would be placed somewhere "beyond the technical level of the junior college and below the professional schools of the University" to study the educational subjects appropriate to the state colleges.[89]

Institutional Organization as a Mode of Critique

California's master plan attempted to strike a balance between accessible and distinctive. To make that balance economically sustainable, the state made the lower division, general education, and the liberal arts the most accessible and least distinctive aspects of its institutions. By investing in multiple UC campuses, California also made resource-intensive inquiry more accessible than it might otherwise have been. California thus grew accessibility at every "level" of education. Christopher Newfield cites that model in his defense of public universities and credits California for implementing what he calls the "inquiry for all" model of higher education, a commitment to provide on a mass scale the opportunity for students "to be exposed to both the *results* of advanced research and the *process* through which research creates new knowledge."[90] Newfield's arguments echo the 1955 restudy, which defined the functions of the UC in strikingly similar terms. It was to instruct "able young people, not merely by transmitting to them established knowledge and skills, but by helping them to experience with their teachers the actual processes."[91]

Writing after the Education Amendment Act of 1972 in a more egalitarian era of higher education, Newfield takes the idea of inquiry-based undergraduate education a step beyond the 1955 restudy. To its recommendations he adds that "research faculty do not see independent inquiry as an add-on or special challenge for only the most gifted students"; rather, they see it "as the destination of undergraduate education overall."[92] The benefit, Newfield argues, of implementing the "inquiry for all" model on a mass scale is that "a much higher proportion" of students attain intellectual independence.[93] It is for that reason, he explains, that UC campuses designate knowledge transmission as "largely the domain of 'lower division' and arrange their upper-division coursework for juniors and seniors to participate directly in research.[94] Newfield does not present the upper division as akin to Eliot's system of electives. He instead argues it as a necessity that gives UC undergraduates an "essential ingredient of the 'lifetime learning' that the contemporary economy is said to require."[95]

Newfield acknowledges that the "inquiry for all" model is as much a pattern of institutional organization as it is a pedagogical model. It requires specialized facilities and coordinated enrollment plans, conditions that California realized by founding not one but ten public research universities. California's community colleges and regional universities, Newfield notes, "have fewer resources" and "offer less or little research" but he does not elaborate on why.[96] And his argument presumes a teaching mission for the UC that never existed, at least not formally. The UC dedicated its 1960 all-faculty conference to detailing the university's research function. That conference argued that research institutions succeeded because other institutions, including the "uniquely American" four-year liberal arts college, were responsible for the bulk of teaching. The "existence of such colleges preserves the university," it concluded.[97] The 1960 UC faculty characterized as "utopian" the hope that a country committed to "supplying higher education to a large portion of its citizens" could "combine major research with teaching."[98] The conference cited the need for specialized equipment and capable personnel in justifying why "academic research must be concentrated in a relatively small proportion of America's institutions of higher education" and separated from teaching.[99] It made no mention at all of its own role in undergraduate education.

Transferring at the Margins of the California Master Plan

The 1989 legislative review of California's Master Plan found that the model failed to meet a state goal set in 1973 to achieve enrollments that reflect the demographics of California's high school graduates.[100] The review found that the Master Plan reinforced systemic inequity by relying on grades as indicators of student potential without considering how some students benefit from academic support and opportunities unavailable to others. The report attributes the enrollment shortfall to the inequitable funding model that allocates fewer resources to the campuses that serve students from the least privileged backgrounds. For the Master Plan to improve access for "persons now in the margins," the report argues, California needs "a more equitable distribution of educational resources among the three systems."[101] It acknowledges that changes to funding may require revisions to "the current distinctions between a teaching and a research institution."[102]

To uphold its commitments to the surrounding region and to address historical inequities, CSUMB had to re-think both the administration of credit transfer and conventional understandings of the "teaching college" and the "college ready" student. Evidence of this conceptual work appears throughout CSUMB's early administrative documents. For instance, a memo regarding transfer students who had completed California's general education requirements discussed how CSUMB's language requirement might benefit student populations that were marginalized elsewhere by California education policies and practices. CSUMB required students to become bilingual and bi-literate to a specified level of competence. The university noted that the requirement could be completed quickly by "many heritage speakers of languages other than English," who "in other educational settings . . . are framed educationally as 'behind.'"[103] CSUMB's unique requirement thus allowed the campus to recognize those language skills "as an asset toward graduation."[104]

When they embarked on designing a new university, CSUMB faculty believed that California's tiered system might be organized differently to the greater benefit of historically underserved populations. CSUMB attempted to address the inequities identified in the 1989 legislative review by refiguring the relationship between teaching and research as historically practiced. For instance, rather than serve as a mid-tier between the community colleges and the UC, CSUMB sought to partner with both UC campuses and with the community colleges in research endeavors.[105] The very idea of such partnerships challenged one of the tenets of California's system: only students who had demonstrated certain kinds of academic achievement would benefit from access to inquiry.[106]

The partnership with the UC never materialized, but CSUMB immediately drafted memorandums of understanding (MOU) with four community colleges: Monterey Peninsula College, Cabrillo College, Gavilan College, and Hartnell College. The MOUs established a cooperative admissions program for freshman and sophomores that facilitated the admission of nontraditional students and ensured juniors a place at CSUMB. Moreover, the university agreed to share facilities and collaborate with community college faculty in planning lower-division course work. CSUMB's agreement with Hartnell College, for instance, included plans to partner in internships, international programs, and a virtual archaeology program.[107]

In addition to challenging California's tiered system of higher education, CSUMB integrated inquiry into its curriculum in the spirit of "inquiry for all." Its approach to research rejected the idea that inquiry is a zero-sum game for California universities that requires strict domains to administer. Its approach exemplifies the notion of endless inquiry. Rather than compete with other institutions over existing domains, CSUMB identified new areas of specialized research such as its own water management practices, the marine canyon just off its own coastline, and the pursuits of its community partners.

CSUMB bucked decades of tradition in California with small administrative interventions and a regional approach to research. The university did not presume that successful credit transfer must rely on standardized curricula or that inquiry should be reserved for a select student population. Even though CSUMB never formed a lasting partnership with the UC nor did it succeed in remaking general education requirements, the changes it did make opened up other possible approaches to organizing higher education. They did so by formally recognizing the kind of work that the CSUs and community colleges had engaged in for years and making that work visible at the policy level.

NOTES

1. Evergreen enjoyed wide leeway to chart its own course. CSUMB, in contrast, had to walk back several design preferences in order to conform to California's master plan.

2. Dean E. Clabaugh, "Planning for The Evergreen State College: History and Progress," (Olympia, WA, June 15, 1970): 2. Malcolm Stilson Archives and Special Collections, The Evergreen State College, Olympia, WA.

3. Dean E. Clabaugh, "The Evergreen State College Developmental Aspects Prior to Appointment of the President," (Olympia, WA: November 25, 1969): 3. Malcolm Stilson Archives and Special Collections, The Evergreen State College, Olympia, WA.

4. "A Vision for Learning: Transforming the Paradigm for Higher Education in the 21st Century," (Seaside, CA: 1997): 91.

5. Ibid., 7.

6. Gerald Shenk (CSUMB faculty in the Division of Social, Behavioral, and Global Studies) in conversation with the author (Seaside, CA: October 10, 2014).

7. Ibid.

8. "A Vision for Learning," 63.

9. "A Vision for Learning," 419. According to CSUMB's 1997 self-study, "It was important to learn, as well, that CSUMB is now putting in place—collaboratively, with nearby community colleges—a student-friendly policy on the issue of articulation and transfer relative to the [University Learning Requirements (ULR)], mapping out the relationship between the CSUMB ULR 'scheme' and the Title 5 general education plan of the CSU system. Since 60 percent of the CSUMB population is transfer students, this is an important step forward, ensuring that the ULRs are not an impediment to serving the very students the institution has committed itself to. We would observe that the emerging policy should be reviewed at some identified point in the future, to ensure that, in the name of ease of transfer, the institution is not also compromising core values. Indeed, that this issue of articulation needs further attention was suggested by the fact that several faculty and administrators called it the most serious problem facing the institution relative to the outside world."

10. Frederick C. Kintzer, *Middleman in Higher Education: Improving Articulation Among High Schools, Community Colleges, and Senior Institutions* (San Francisco: Jossey-Bass Publishers, 1973), 1.

11. California Intersegmental Articulation Council, *California Articulation Policies and Procedures Handbook* (2006): 3.

12. Arthur M. Cohen, "The Community Colleges and the Path to the Baccalaureate," (Berkeley, CA: Center for Studies in Higher Education, 2003): 11.

13. Don Hossler, Doug Shapiro, Afet Dundar, Mary Ziskin, Jin Chen, Desiree Zerquera, and Vasti Torres, "Transfer & Mobility: A National View of the Pre-Degree Student Movement in Postsecondary Institutions," (National Student Clearinghouse Research Center, 2012): 5. Students transfer for many different reasons and their movements can be unpredictable. Several 1960s and 1970s studies drew attention to the phenomenon of "reverse" transfers, or students who, for a variety of reasons, transferred from a four-year school to a community college. Kintzer, *Middleman in Higher Education*, 3.

14. McConnell and Holy, "A Restudy of the Needs of California," 122; Kintzer, *Middleman in Higher Education*, 30.

15. Carrie B. Kisker, Arthur M. Cohen, and Richard L. Wagoner, *Reforming Transfer and Articulation in California: Four Statewide Solutions for Creating A More Successful and Seamless Transfer Path to the Baccalaureate* (Los Angeles, CA: Center for the Study of Community Colleges, 2010), v.

16. Paul Westmeyer, *An Analytic History of American Higher Education* (Springfield, IL: Charles C. Thomas, 1997), 89.

17. William Rainey Harper, *The Prospects of the Small College* (Chicago: University of Chicago Press, 1900), 26, 34.

18. Carl G. Winter, "History of the Junior College Movement in California," Bureau of Junior College Education Release 20 (Sacramento, CA: 1964): 9.

19. James L. Wattenberger and Allen A. Witt, "Origins of the California System: How the Junior College Movement Came to California," *Community College Review* 22, no. 4 (1995): 22.

20. Wattenbargar, "Origins of the California System," 22; Kintzer, *Middleman in Higher Education*, 12.

21. Leslie Koltai, *Redefining the Associate Degree* (Washington, DC: American Association of Community and Junior Colleges, 1984).

22. Christopher Jencks and David Riesman, *The Academic Revolution* (Chicago: University of Chicago Press, 1968), 481; Carnegie Commission on Higher Education, "A Chance to Learn: An Action Agenda for Equal Opportunity in Higher Education," (Hightstown NJ: McGraw-Hill, 1970): 12; Adult Education Act Silver Anniversary, 1966–1991 (Washington, DC: Clearinghouse Division of Adult Education and Literacy, 1991), 1. Jencks and Riseman estimate that a handful of junior colleges opened before WWI, and a little over two hundred were in operation at the opening of WWII. According to the Carnegie Commission on Higher Education, by 1968, seven states—California, Florida, Illinois, Michigan, New York, Texas, and Washington—accounted for two-thirds of all community college enrollments and over one-third of all community colleges. Passage of the Economic Opportunity Act of 1964, which established the Adult Basic Education Program, may also have fueled community college growth in the second half of the twentieth century. The federal legislation motivated states to develop adult education plans. The programs established through those plans impacted adult education profoundly. More than 245,000 individuals enrolled in basic education programs in 1966 alone and over the years moved greater numbers of people toward a GED.

23. Susan H. Frost, "Historical and Philosophical Foundations for Academic Advising," *Academic Advising: A Comprehensive Handbook*, Ed. Virginia N. Gordon, Wesley R. Habley, and Associates (San Francisco: Jossey-Bass, 2000), 11; Koltai, *Redefining the Associate Degree*, 4.

24. Kintzer, *Middleman in Higher Education*, 5. Kintzer also explains that until 1983 when the legislature issued guidelines, Washington's colleges and universities developed "voluntary and cooperative" agreements with each other on a case-by-case basis. In his 1970 report, Clabaugh reported that Evergreen's first board of trustees signaled an early commitment to coordination and articulation in two if its first five goals: "the integration of urban-rural educational experiences in a regional environment affording a high degree of cultural, social and economic diversification" and "integrated and complimentary relationship to existing and future patterns of higher education in the state." Kintzer, *Middleman in Higher Education*, 92; Clabaugh, "Planning for The Evergreen State College," 3.

25. Richard S. Mosholder and Christopher J. Zirkle, "Historical Trends of Articulation in America: A Review of the Literature," *Community College Journal of Research and Practice* 31, no. 9 (2007): 740.

26. Carnegie Commission, "A Chance to Learn," 19. The Carnegie Commission on Higher Education 1970 report on community colleges urged universities to give qualified transfer students priority whenever faced with enrollment restrictions and not to discriminate against transfer students when allocating financial aid.

27. Kintzer, *Middleman in Higher Education*, 144. Kintzer further explains that Florida, the first state to implement a statewide transfer agreement for general education requirements, did so with a tiered administrative model that other states adopted. After the Florida State Board of Education in 1965 approved an articulation agreement guaranteeing community college students acceptance at public universities, the state established a coordinating committee to oversee the agreements. Each of the universities likewise appointed external and internal relations officers to manage everyday transfer processes. Kintzer, *Middleman in Higher Education*, 35; see also: Quentin J. Bogart and Sue I. Murphey, "Articulation in a Changing Higher Education Environment," *Community College Review* 13, no.2 (1985): 18.

28. McConnell, "A Restudy of the Needs of California," 122.

29. Ibid.

30. Bogart, "Articulation," 20.

31. Herta Teitelbaum, "Anticipating, Implementing, and Adapting to Changes in Academic Advising." *Academic Advising: A Comprehensive Handbook*. Ed. Virginia N. Gordon, Wesley R. Habley, and Associates. (San Francisco: Jossey-Bass, 2000), 400.

32. Catherine Minicucci, "An Evaluation of the Transfer Center Pilot Program, Volume 1," (Berkeley, CA: Berman, Weiler Associates, 1989); Mosholder "Historical Trends of Articulation."

33. Elena Silva, Taylor White, and Thomas Toch, "The Carnegie Unit: A Century-Old Standard in a Changing Education Landscape," (Stanford, CA: Carnegie Foundation for the Advancement of Teaching, 2015): 30.

34. Ronnald W. Farland, "Proposals for Strengthening the Associate Degree in the California Community Colleges" (1985); Ronnald W. Farland and Connie Anderson. "Transfer and Articulation with Four-Year Colleges and Universities: A Report," (Sacramento: Office of the Chancellor, California Community Colleges, 1989).

35. Quentin J. Bogart and Sue I. Murphey, "Articulation in a Changing Higher Education Environment," *Community College Review* 13, no. 2 (1985): 21.

36. Hans Johnson, "Higher Education in California: New Goals for the Master Plan," (San Francisco: Public Policy Institute of California, 2010), 4–5.

37. John Vasconcellos and the Joint Committee for Review of the Master Plan for Higher Education, "California Faces . . . California's Future: Education for Citizenship in a Multicultural Democracy" (Sacramento: California State Assembly, 1989): 32.

38. Ibid., 36, 39.

39. Administration of credit transfer remains complex enough that it still requires dedicated staff positions and software programs such as "assist.org" and "degree progress." See: http://admission.universityofcalifornia.edu/transfer/preparation-paths/index.html

40. Donald R. Gerth, *The People's University: A History of the California State University* (CA: Berkeley Public Policy Press, 2010), 15. The question of a common academic calendar was raised again in 1963 by the Coordinating Council, which sought to bring the three systems into a shared calendar. Morgan Odell, "Distribution of Authority with the California State College System," (PhD dissertation, University of Southern California, 1967).

41. Carnegie Foundation for the Advancement of Teaching, "State Higher Education in California," (Sacramento: California State Printing Office, 1932), 32.

42. Gerth, *People's University*, 84.

43. Lyman A. Glenny, *Autonomy of the Public Colleges: The Challenge of Coordination* (New York, NY: McGraw-Hill, 1959), 209.

44. Odell, "Distribution of Authority," 103–05.

45. Carnegie Foundation for the Advancement of Teaching, "State Higher Education in California," (Sacramento: California State Printing Office, 1932), 47–48. Emphasis in the original.

46. Ibid., 16, 15.

47. Ibid., 43.

48. Ibid.

49. Ibid., 37. The question of whether community colleges should replicate the lower division of the university or instead offer comparable courses was never settled. By the 1950s, a trend toward comparable courses had replaced the replication policy that Lange established in the early twentieth century, but Kintzer documents the findings of educational reports that suggest the practice continued. A 1970 Carnegie Commission on Higher Education report on community colleges echoed the 1932 report and encouraged specializations at the community colleges when regional or local interests made a case for it. It also clarified that the colleges should offer different types of associate degrees including occupational degrees in addition to transferrable degrees. Kintzer, *Middleman in Higher Education*, 13; Carnegie Commission, "A Chance to Learn," 16–17, 47.

50. Carnegie Foundation, "State Higher Education," 60.

51. Ibid.

52. Ibid., 16.

53. Ibid., 23.

54. Ibid., 24.

55. Ibid., 21.

56. Ibid., 40.

57. Ibid., 54.

58. Ibid.

59. Ibid., 41.

60. Gerth, *People's University*, 34. Until the 1920 Legislature abolished local boards, Odell suggests that local boards had "a rather proprietary attitude toward their schools" born of the "vigorous local effort" behind the founding of each college." Odell, "Distribution of Authority," 101.

61. Gerth, *People's University*, 84.

62. Monroe E. Deutsch, Aubrey A. Douglass, and George D. Strayer, "Report of a Survey of the Needs of California in Higher Education," (1948): 65.

63. Ibid.

64. Ibid., 22.

65. Ibid., 36–37.

66. Ibid., 40.

67. Gerth, *People's University*, 91. See also Gerth's description of how that conversation unfolded among the state colleges which had inconsistent representation during deliberations. Gerth, *People's University*, 88.

68. Deutsch, "Report of a Survey," 31.

69. Gerth, *People's University*, 93, 98.

70. McConnell, "A Restudy of the Needs," 58–59. The 1955 restudy also encouraged more experimentation at the junior colleges, which the authors suggested had "not given the national leadership in general education that they might have." The authors found the junior colleges more concerned with ensuring "that the transfer student's background is equivalent to a student's who has completed his lower-division work at the University" and that general education offerings "conform to the attitude and practice of the University of California."

71. McConnell, "A Restudy of the Needs," 66.

72. Ibid., 64.

73. Ibid., 66.

74. Odell, "Distribution of Authority."

75. McConnell, "A Restudy of the Needs," 95.

76. Ibid.

77. John B. Barnes and Gerald R. Reed, Eds. *The Emerging State College: Boise State College Seminar Dialogue* (Boise, ID: Monograph No. 1, 1969), 19.

78. George A. Gries, "Agricultural Programs in California Public Higher Education," (Sacramento: California State Coordinating Council for Higher Education, 1971), 56.

79. Ibid., 55.

80. Ibid., 120.

81. Ibid., xxxiv.

82. Ibid.

83. Ibid., 91.

84. Ibid., 66.

85. California State Colleges, *Biennium Report of State Colleges to State Board of Education* (September 15, 1946). In 1946, San Jose State College proposed programs in police training in the Department of Justice Studies.

86. McConnell, "A Restudy of the Needs," 78. As explained in the 1955 Restudy: "Economy dictates that the libraries and laboratories necessary for their research, and for the instruction of their students, be concentrated in a few centers. . . . Experience teaches that all four functions of a university—research, teaching, professional training, public service—are best carried out in institutions that bring together in a single intellectual community active workers in the most diverse fields, so that each can avail himself freely of the stimulus and the aid (generally unpredictable, but sometimes decisive) that he may need from experts in other areas of learning." McConnell, "A Restudy of the Needs," 78–79.

87. McConnell, "A Restudy of the Needs," 89–90. The 1955 committee continued to struggle with the question of how best to organize the various domains of education: "In one continuum, differences in emphasis may relate to the theoretical versus the practical, or fundamental versus applied. In the field of agriculture, for example, the junior colleges should emphasize the attainment of techniques which the skilled worker will need. The state colleges should stress a combination of theory and practice leading to an understanding of basic principles as well as the acquisition of technical abilities. Vocational performance, nevertheless, is a

primary objective of this type of program. Finally, University curriculums in agriculture should place still greater emphasis on theoretical considerations with stress on the scientific phases of agriculture."

88. Vasconcellos, "California Faces," 12.

89. Deutsch, "Report of a Survey," 31.

90. Christopher Newfield, *Unmaking the Public University: The Forty-Year Assault on the Middle Class* (Cambridge, MA: Harvard University Press, 2008), 190–91. [Emphasis in the original.]

91. McConnell, "A Restudy of the Needs," 74.

92. Newfield, *Unmaking*, 191.

93. Ibid.

94. Ibid., 190.

95. Ibid., 191.

96. Ibid., 190.

97. University of California, Berkeley All-University Faculty Conference. "The Research Function of the University: Proceedings," (Riverside: University of California, 1960), 9.

98. Ibid., 8.

99. Ibid., 9.

100. Vasconcellos, "California Faces," 18. The report cites 1986 enrollment numbers when "fewer than 900 black high school graduates in our entire state are eligible for the University of California, when only 674 Black and Latino persons transfer from the 106 Community Colleges into the University of California, and when only 4,468 Blacks and Latinos are among the 27,761 Californians who transfer into the California State University." Vasconcellos, "California Faces," 8.

101. Ibid., 5, 17.

102. Ibid., 12.

103. "University Learning Requirements" (June 1996), Manuscript No. 1, Box 2, Series 1, File 75, Folder ii. Armando Arias Archive. Tanimura & Antle Family Memorial Library Archives and Special Collections, California State University Monterey Bay, Seaside, CA.

104. Ibid.

105. A March 1993 press release from CSUMB announced a "multiuniversity redevelopment effort" that would "include a joint CSU/UC educational and research center." Manuscript No. 1, Box 7, Series 8, File 9. Armando Arias Archive. Tanimura & Antle Family Memorial Library Archives and Special Collections, California State University Monterey Bay, Seaside, CA.

106. William Chance, "A Vision in Progress: The Decision to Establish a Public University at Monterey Bay," (San Jose, CA: California Higher Education Policy Center, 1997): 25. CSUMB joined four well-established community colleges serving the tri-county area: Hartnell College, a private institution founding in 1920 in Salinas, Monterey Peninsula College, a public institution established in 1947 in Monterey, Cabrillo College, established in 1959 in Aptos, and Gavilan College, established as San Benito County Junior College in 1919 in Gilroy. Those campuses stood to lose students to the new university. The university promised to "coordinate pre-admissions procedures so that CSU-eligible students attending any of the community colleges in the Tri-County region can be pre-admitted to CSUMB."

107. "Accord of Mutual Collaboration: A Partnership Between Hartnell College's Social Sciences Department and CSUMB's Center for Social and Behavioral Sciences" (December 12, 1996). Manuscript No. 1, Box 1, Series 1, File 13—Articulation, 1996–1999. Armando Arias Archive. Tanimura & Antle Family Memorial Library Archives and Special Collections, California State University Monterey Bay, Seaside, CA.

Conclusion

An Assemblage of Possibilities

The California Legislature passed the 2010 Student Transfer Achievement Reform Act (SB 1440) with good intentions. The law aims to make college less cumbersome, more accessible, and less expensive by minimizing the bureaucratic hassles of credit transfer. Traditional articulation agreements transfer credits on a course-by-course basis. SB 1440 transfers the entire lower division as a single package. SB 1440 requires community colleges to grant "an associate degree for transfer" once a student has met specified general education and major requirements. The law then guarantees those students admission to the CSU, which is prohibited from requiring a student to repeat courses similar to those that counted toward the associate degree. Lawmakers hoped that reducing bureaucratic headaches would improve graduation rates and lower the cost to the state of educating each student. The law's principal author, Senator Alex Padilla, justified the intervention by citing two common practices that discourage students from graduating: frequent changes to degree requirements and duplicative course work.[1] His concerns were warranted. Students bear the time and expense of non-transferrable classes when they must take courses similar to those they have already completed. When complicated transfer policies converge with enrollment requirements and financial aid restrictions, students often become just frustrated enough to delay graduation or discontinue their studies. SB 1440 reduces the likelihood of that happening by instituting reliable and consistent channels between the community colleges and the CSU.

SB 1440 is the legacy of California's master plan. The new law reflects the historical association between accessibility, enrollment, and transferability that differentiated function established. From its first iteration, the Plan

113

imagined higher education as structured by standardized channels in which the community colleges and the CSUs served as supports for the UCs. The Master Plan meant for the community colleges and the CSUs to accommodate, affordably, a much larger number of students than the UCs, which could then focus on research. When measured against the goals California's Master Plan, SB 1440 is a sensible approach to education insofar as it makes a four-year degree cheaper and easier to obtain.

The new law illustrates the ways in which California's master plan has been a self-fulfilling prophecy. The community colleges and the California State colleges were still sovereign campuses when California adopted the plan. SB 1440 is the latest step in the decades-long effort to erase the differences between those campuses, a feat it accomplishes by treating all lower-division coursework as interchangeable. The ethnographic details that I have shared in this project suggest it is unlikely that the individual classes themselves are indistinguishable. The newest transfer legislation follows generations of education reforms where it treats those minute differences as problems to resolve rather than resources to cultivate. That work is often done in the name of accessibility and without consideration for the situated practices that enrich teaching and inquiry.

The overall structure of California higher education conveys a broad sense of accessibility. By breaking the academic project into pieces and distributing it across systems and campuses, the state has amassed a wealth of resources that collectively offer academic breadth. Yet, to administer that system, California has operated with a much narrower sense of "accessible." For the community colleges and the CSUs, for instance, accessible means that a person can live in any populated area of the state and attend a degree-granting institution. It does not mean that students have access to any area of study. It does not mean the availability of different curricular models. It does not mean "inquiry for all," as Newfield suggests, nor does it mean that every campus has extensive libraries, laboratories, and studios or even the means to secure such resources. Neither does it mean that each college and university has access to a full range of student populations.

California's overarching goal was to build a sustainable system that ensured education as a readily available public resource. That dream met from the outset with the realities of higher education's existing infrastructure: a collection of academic institutions each with distinct missions, curricula, and features. California initially embraced that institutional diversity and then systematized it. It grouped schools together and delimited their practices. It separated inquiry from teaching so as to avoid the complexities of the one from interfering with the administration of the other. The approach effectively resolved philosophical differences by codifying a division of labor. The Master Plan has since answered all curricular, pedagogical, methodological, and administrative questions with the concept of differentiated functions.

When asked whether the state would benefit from multiple agricultural schools, the answer lay in the Plan, which discouraged redundancy and gave priority to University of California campuses. When the question concerned appropriate funding levels for undergraduate education, the answer lay in the Plan, which determined that graduate programs required more funds for specialized research (just as Hall had argued years before). If the question was whether undergraduates could design a personal course of study (as Eliot advocated), or whether campuses should contribute to the betterment of neighboring communities (as Bascom proposed), California's system of differentiated functions answered: no and maybe. It makes sense within the logic of the Master Plan to consider first and foremost whether any campus modification, such as lower-division service learning classes, violates the differentiations the policy institutes. The concept of differentiated function has simplified research, for instance, by restricting where it occurs and by organizing into a single consistent form. It recently answered the question of whether the CSUs could offer doctorates by authorizing the CSU to award only a doctor of education degree (EdD).[2] It then answered the question of whether an EdD was equivalent to a PhD by stipulating that EdD students complete their degrees three years from the time they are admitted, half the time granted on average to UC students earning PhDs.[3]

Buried under California educational policies are the alternative models that educational projects have supplied over the years, such as CSUMB's research partnerships with neighboring community colleges. Beneath the differentiated functions that each campus enacts, other possible educational futures lay dormant. California's master plan preserved the basic pattern of U.S. higher education by retaining a collection of separate campuses, but its governance approach has emptied that structure of its critical capacity. The fact that individual campuses have continued modifying the academic project—adding a viniculture degree in the central valley, establishing the nation's first feminist art program and departments of ethnic studies—suggests that California's answers to educational questions are inadequate.[4] California's master plan, in other words, has never settled the question of who gets to study what, with which resources, for how long, and at what value. More important, the Master Plan obscures the answers that other projects generate. It eclipses their implications and the additional questions they provoke. Where its own policies make it difficult to see the stakes of educational debates; when the deliberations drop from sight, the Master Plan falls short of securing Californians full access to the academic project.

We cannot engage with educational ideas that we cannot see. In California's case, its system of differentiated functions makes it difficult to see how institutional diversity might serve a critical modality. When schools are evaluated by how well they comply with the state's plan, alternative practices register as confusion and dysfunction rather than educational critique. Equally concerning is the impression made by inflexible policies and practices that cast existing infrastructure as inevitable, necessary, or interchangeable. That approach presumes all schools share a fundamental core that can only be either degraded or further refined. That belief has set the stage for two different yet complementary reform movements. The first movement seeks to restrict access to educational resources by intensifying institutions' differentiated functions. The second movement aims to liberate education from its institutions and disperse it throughout social practice. Though the two efforts move in opposite directions, they share a dislike of institutional excess. Both view higher education's complexity as a problem born of cumbersome and gratuitous infrastructure.

Bill Readings has argued that a vague pursuit of excellence underwrites the movement to restrict access to higher education.[5] Those who advocate stricter admissions polices and who oppose "inquiry for all" treat excellence as a finite resource threatened by the demands of mass education. The pursuit of excellence underwrites the belief that college is not for everyone and it questions whether every student really needs general education. Some reformers also question whether academia has exhausted inquiry's frontier with too much specialization and with research conducted merely for the sake of professional success.[6] Stanford University president John Hennessy typified this thinking when he warned that higher education had strained its limited resources beyond what was sustainable. "[W]e are simply trying to support too many universities that are trying to be research institutions," Hennessy told *The New Yorker* in 2013. "Nationally," he continued, "we may not be able to afford as many research institutions going forward."[7] Hennessy treats research as a zero-sum game, but Eliot and Hall might have been skeptical of Hennessy's claim about institutional strain. Both argued that even exceptional students and wealthy schools had only so much space, time, and attention to study all that the world contained. Their approaches considered how best to distribute that work. Hall, for instance, built a research university with few disciplines and a handful of faculty because he believed that inquiry required attention to the tiniest of details. His approach invited the kind of distributed models of inquiry that Evergreen and CSUMB have attempted.

Hennessy's conclusions correspond with California's tiered organizational model. The state's policy of differentiated functions likewise presumes that the inquiries underway at some schools are too insignificant to be worthwhile. California policymakers operationalized that belief when they decided that research universities could only take one form. The policies that reserve inquiry as the UC's domain are another self-fulfilling prophecy. They justify under-resourcing other campuses. The decision to position the EdD beneath the PhD follows from that line of thinking as does the unwillingness to recognize service learning as a form of scholarship. The approach departs from Hall's belief that even the tiniest contributions to inquiry matter. When the scholarly contributions of some campuses go unrecognized, they become insignificant.

A second reform movement, one exemplified by Carey's University of Everywhere, stems from a deep skepticism of any form of school. Like Hennessy, Carey does not see institutions as generative. But where Hennessy finds some schools merely inadequate, Carey argues them unnecessary. To Carey, the collection of brick and mortar campuses that make up U.S. higher education are at best an analog prototype that we have outgrown. Carey sees only limitations and outdated technologies. His opposition to traditional admissions processes, for instance, stems from his belief that education is limited by physical constraints. "As long as elite institutions are bound to physical places," he argues, "they will only ever touch a tiny sliver of humanity."[8] His is a version of the Wisconsin Idea scaled up to accommodate billions of people. It includes a radical variation on Eliot's inquiry-by-personal pursuit. If higher education became available to billions of people, he argues, those billions would in turn "create large amounts of electronic data," which will fuel "unprecedented analyses of human learning."[9]

Carey's ideas likewise correspond with the California model. His reforms align with the belief that educational content can become interchangeable and its delivery made seamless. California's refinement of credit transfer (e.g., SB 1440) is the kind of technocratic fix that Carey might appreciate even if he still found it outdated and inadequate. In Carey's version of higher education, competency-based learning would eliminate the need for credit hours and evidence of student achievement would detach from institutions altogether, free finally to travel with the student wherever they go.

As divergent as their proposals are, Hennessy and Carey have faith that we will never lose sight of higher education. Both trust that it will remain conspicuous whether it becomes more restrictive or ubiquitous. No matter whether it becomes more refined, merges with industry, or loses its pomp and old-time college style, we will still see it and know it as higher education.

The California model serves as a cautionary tale for such reform movements. Going smaller or bigger without understanding how either might obscure educational complexities runs the risk of damaging the resources that make higher education worthwhile. The fixes that Hennessy and Carey promise might only exacerbate the obscurity that higher education suffers. Reserving inquiry for a select few will not ensure its value. Making college available to as many people as possible will not demystify it. Those reforms will make it harder to see educational choices and consider other possibilities. The loss of visibility spells the loss of critical capacities. At risk is the chance to ask why education is structured as it is. Why this requirement, this admissions practice, this selection of readings? Visibility is the prerequisite for disputing and modifying education's form.

The challenge for advocates is how to nurture that visibility without overwhelming the debates with details. Education always risks appearing messy and unwieldy the closer we look. It is easier and safer to argue, as I have done here, how macro educational systems foreclose on other possibilities. The value of keeping alternative approaches in sight seems to diminish the more we look to smaller classroom-level actions. At best, those situated practices will seem too idiosyncratic to sustain (to many reformers, the institutional details always seem expendable). At worst, they will appear the inevitable effect of systemic designs. How to present them instead as the dynamic constitutive force they are and the means by which education remakes itself?

One way of doing that is by valuing situated-ness as an achievement in and of itself. It is a matter of shifting from a situational orientation to a situational sensibility. In communication education, generic approaches to instruction tend to equate familiar forms with quality messaging. When communication is taught as a series of oversimplified principles, students associate normative communication styles with competency and attempt to master a set of privileged techniques that promise to convey any message no matter the content. Critics of the generic approach have addressed its shortcomings with tailored instruction that asks students to adapt their style to different situations. That approach represents a situational orientation that does not necessarily foster a situational sensibility. Nussbaum's survey of U.S. philosophy classes exhibits that orientation insofar as she assumes educators can adopt different instructional approaches while teaching the same stable core body of knowledge. A situational sensibility differs from a situational orientation in that it recognizes situations as generative educational accomplishments in their own right rather than variations on the same premise. That distinction can be difficult to discern when the accomplishment takes the form of a slight variation. Moreover, it is difficult to articulate the value of such an accomplishment in the policy spheres where decisions happen. I repeatedly experienced that challenge while assembling this project and found myself asking, what am I looking for?

A question that I posed to Evergreen and CSUMB faculty further illustrates the challenge. I asked whether it mattered to them that their campuses were state schools. Several of the answers described the school's relationship to the state in terms of sight. Rita Pougiales, Evergreen's former dean of hiring, observed that a school's public status gives educators an audience with other public bodies such as a legislature. Being public, she explained, meant having "the potential to influence" and to add "a voice and perspective" to discussions about what education should be.[10] Another Evergreen faculty member made a similar comment saying that she felt being public might not be significant at this point if no one knows what a school does. "Academics," she observed, "haven't done a good job of staying connected to the state. You know, out of sight out of mind kind of thing."[11]

These answers clarified the question that sits at the heart of this project: How do educators show others what we want them to see in academic institutions and in our work? That question sat at the edge of my thoughts while I visited both campuses and struggled to articulate what it was I hoped to see. The first time I sat in on a class (a course on elementary education) I noted how hard it was not to treat my visit as a teaching observation. I did not know what to record. Since it was not my intent to advocate an Evergreen or a CSUMB model, I was not there to find proof of concept. I was not searching for best practices. The discussions, materials, and activities were enchanting, and also distracting, but I could not say what they distracted from. As I struggled with that question, I kept circling back to Dan Fernandez's banana bread.

Fernandez is a member of the CSUMB faculty and was chair of the Division of Science and Environmental Policy when I spoke with him. He shared the details of one of his "pet projects" related to sustainability: baking banana bread in a solar oven on a patio attached to CSUMB's Chapman Science Academic Center, the university's first new building.[12] Fernandez mixes the bread batter in the building's kitchenette and at certain times of the year, the sun hits the patio long enough to bake it. "Over the summer it will be in the sun till about four, so that gives me more daylight hours. But I can bake in the winter. I baked on solstice, winter solstice."[13] He then shares the bread with colleagues and students who marvel that it came from a solar oven. I appreciated Fernandez's banana bread as a creative teaching strategy and an ingenious way to promote the science division. I was struck above all by the circumstances that came together to make that bread: a personal interest combined with a specific body of expertise; an investment on the part of the university in environmental studies and sustainability; the funding (at long last) for a science building at CSUMB; the open patio and Fernandez's observations of how the sun moved across it.

The banana bread offered a vivid example of what educators accomplish when interests, training, professional commitments, and institutional resources converge. That insight at first seemed to be the story's sole significance. The banana bread was a memorable convergence that illustrated the variety and texture in academic practice. I encountered another memorable convergence in a proposed year-long seminar for first-year students that Sarah Pedersen designed with a documentary filmmaker and an evolutionary biologist. Pedersen is faculty at Evergreen and was the Dean of Library and Media Services when I first spoke with her. As originally conceived, "Between Land and Sea" would explore scientific, literary, and visual ways of telling the story of change; it would incorporate maritime studies and feminist theory; it would consider metaphorical and literal borders in literacy genres and Pacific coastlines; it would include two sailing trips in the Puget Sound.[14] The program's design attended to the possibilities of convergence at both the curricular and pedagogical level. It composed its conditions from an unusual association of materials and built a sequence of spaces in which students could forge their own connections, or as the course description put it, gain a sense for how "vision and insight are intertwined."[15]

Just as I saw resourcefulness in Fernandez's baking, I saw in "Between Land and Sea" a flair for finding creative ways of arranging instruction and inquiry to generate new fields of study. What was not yet apparent in these examples was how they might support a more fundamental shift in higher education from a situational orientation to a sustained sensibility.

I gradually realized that my sense of these two examples as exceptional limited their significance. Like the investment in excellence that Readings questions, exceptionalism discourages the conceptual leap from orientation to sensibility. Communication-in-the-disciplines programs (a variation on the more generic communication-across-the-curriculum) face the same challenge when they embed communication instruction in a particular discipline or major.[16] Embedded programs do not necessarily foster an appreciation for the possibilities that situated-ness presents. They can instead deepen the impression that situated-ness represents limitations.[17] Educational advocates risk a similar impression when we treat situated differences as representative exemplars of a regional mission or an alternative pedagogy. By that account, Fernandez's banana bread and Pedersen's tour of the surrounding landscape represent little more than a pedagogical approach attuned to the local environment. Speaking to this dilemma, Muckelbauer distinguishes between an instructional approach that aims to document stylistic differences (and employ them in appropriate settings), and an approach that "[provokes] an inhabitation" and an "immanent connection."[18] The former adds complexity to the communication course but does not modify its precepts. The latter, Muckelbauer explains, "is structured by its own capacity to transform."[19] It is an approach that takes seriously what Lave calls education's "stickiness."[20]

I began this project hoping to show education's inventive capacity by finding instructional materials so unusual they would evidence distinct contributions to knowledge worthy of funding. I gradually realized that my goal was the conceptual equivalent of arguing the value of different communication styles. Both hold onto the hope that all our messy practices share a coherent core. In the end, exemplars were not what I needed. *I needed a sense of higher education as inhabited situations.* I finally encountered that sense in an Evergreen class that demanded I engage it on its own terms. That class afforded me a chance to experience educational accomplishment as radical instability.

In the fall of 2014, I caught up with Pedersen's seminar, "Between Land and Sea." The seminar did not run as originally planned. Andrew Buchman, a musician and musicologist, had joined in place of a documentarian. By October, the class had completed its first sailing trip and they were working through poetry, evolutionary biology, and learning to make soundscapes. I accompanied Buchman to lunch one day in the student union and sat with students from the class. Some told me they were attracted to the course by their love of animals. One student said she took the course out of a love of both animals and singing. Buchman asked her if she might sing a song about the shore and would she lend her voice to the soundscapes scheduled for Wednesday? She thought of a song and sang. In the days leading up to the soundscapes, Buchman prompted other students to make contributions to Wednesday's class. Would you bring your squeezebox? Would you choreograph a dance? On the eve of class he learned that the piano would be newly tuned just in time. Wednesday was taking shape before my eyes.

Wednesday morning we met in the Communications Building. Students arrived early to rehearse. Class began. The first performance was a ballet that a student had choreographed to "Hebrides Overture," which the class had listened to the previous week. A song on accordion followed the ballet, then a wind chorus, and Buchman playing piano. Someone demonstrated the digital audio editor by splicing together the recordings they just made. One of the sample recordings included an image of birds on a guitar. A student asked about the birds and a voice spoke up from the back of the room. "They are zebra finches. Bred to be domesticated." Someone asked how to avoid the normalization feature. She would like her recording to sound natural, she explained. In the pause while the demonstration wrapped up, a student told the class that she had found a 16 mm documentary called "Beyond Land and Sea" in the film archive under the library stairs and would like to share it at a future date. Another accordion performance followed. This time the student played and sang sea shanties from a book he had found. The second half of class was a presentation by Micah McCarty, a Makah tribal council leader and an artist. He spoke about Makah aesthetics and canoe technology while he demonstrated form line drawing. His comments moved back and forth between discussion of drawing technique, a history of treaties with Indigenous peoples broken in the name of environmentalism, and descriptions of reoccurring animal figures in Makah stories. When he asked for animals to draw, Pedersen suggested the animals that students were researching. Students called out names. Platypus. Heron. Puffin. Octopus. The form line drawings gradually filled the back wall of the auditorium.

What was it about that class that helped me to distinguish a situational orientation from a sensibility? My notes listed themes and identified the areas of study the class incorporated. I registered different pedagogical styles. Why were those my notes? Did I intend to showcase what distinguished it from more conventional classes? Did I hope to cite those details to affirm it as education? None of the idiosyncrasies of that day now strike me as significant beyond the ways they gestured at each turn to all the other directions the class might have taken. In the end, only the unsettledness of the activities stayed with me. Each piece of the class had brought to mind questions. What is the lesson in this sea shanty? Did anyone else catch a connection between McCarty's comments about environmentalism and the wish that recordings sound natural? What do art and music appreciation lend to the study of animals?

The unsettledness of that class was conspicuous but not unique. As might happen in any classroom, instructors and students assembled a collection of materials, ideas, and activities. An odd assortment of comments, explanations, questions, and gestures stitched together the pieces. Students expressed interests and aspirations. Some moments stretched out and others struggled to gain purchase. Each contribution seemed capable of carrying us in multiple directions. We all briefly inhabited the form that emerged. Some parts of it felt familiar and others drifted from convention. For a moment I caught a glimpse of an assemblage of possibilities that hinted at education's future forms.

Much of the work that has gone into designing and administering schools is animated by a curiosity for those unimagined unrealized forms. As higher education reorganizes itself amidst shifting political commitments and emergent technologies, it must decide whether or not to sustain its historic curiosity for possibility. But first we have to want to recognize those possibilities in academia's existing infrastructure. It is easy to see it all instead as dead ends and headaches, impasses and sinkholes, or a fatal combination of too much and too little. If we are willing to look closely, we can see instead the vivid details of classes and inquiries unfolding into distinct projects, each one iterative, conditional, partial, and unsettled.

NOTES

1. https://collegecampaign.org/wp-content/uploads/2014/06/2010_11_04_CCO_SB1440_Fact_Sheet.pdf

2. Senate Bill No. 724 describes the authorization as an exception to the state's differentiation of function codified in the Master Plan (93). Prior to the passage of SB 724, the UC had exclusive jurisdiction in California public higher education to award the doctoral degree. An exception was made to meet the state's urgent need for qualified public school administrators.

3. Executive Order 991: Doctor of Education Degree Programs:https://calstate.policystat.com/policy/6591243/latest/#autoid-344mx

4. Judy Chicago launched a five course Feminist Art Program in 1971 at Fresno State College (now California State University, Fresno). A student strike at San Francisco State University in 1968 led to the establishment of the first ethnic studies department in the U.S.

5. Bill Readings, *The University in Ruins* (Cambridge, MA: Harvard University Press, 1996).

6. Stanley Fish, *Doing What Comes Naturally: Change, Rhetoric, and the Practice of Theory in Literary and Legal Studies* (Durham, NC: Duke University Press, 1989), 203. Stanley Fish responded to the complaint of too much research activity by characterizing it as "a strange crisis, since [robust research activity] bears all the marks of disciplinary health."

7. Nathan Heller, "Laptop U: Has the Future of College Moved Online?" *The New Yorker* 20 (May 2013): 85.

8. Kevin Carey, *The End of College: Creating the Future of Learning and the University of Everywhere* (New York: Riverhead Books, 2016), 215.

9. Carey, *The End of College*, 225.

10. Rita Pougiales (Evergreen faculty and former Dean of hiring) in conversation with the author (Olympia, WA, April 24, 2013).

11. Evergreen faculty in conversation with the author (Olympia, WA, October 21, 2013).

12. Dan Fernandez (CSUMB faculty and former chair of the Division of Science and Environmental Policy) in conversation with the author (Seaside, CA, November 19, 2012).

13. Ibid.

14. Sarah Pedersen (Evergreen faculty and former Dean of Library and Media Services) in conversation with the author (Olympia, WA, April 25, 2013).

15. The Evergreen State College 2014–15 Catalog, 37.

16. Ann L. Darling and Deanna P. Dannels, "Practicing Engineers Talk about the Importance of Talk: A Report on the Role of Oral Communication in the Workplace," *Communication Education* 52, no. 1(2003): 1–16.

17. Deanna P. Dannels, "Communication across the Curriculum Problematics and Possibilities: Standing at the Forefront of Educational Reform," *The Sage Handbook of Communication and Instruction*, Eds. Deanna L. Fassett & John T. Warren (Thousand Oaks, CA: Sage, 2010), 55–79. This criticism can take many forms. Some disciplines, for instance, might invite embedded lessons in communication and then resist the instructional approaches that support a tailored approach.

18. Muckelbaur, *Future of Invention*, 137, 140.

19. Ibid., 140.

20. Lave, *Apprenticeship*, 18.

Bibliography

"1st Progress Report, Watershed Ecology Outreach Program," (Moss Landing Marine Laboratories, Benthic Lab, September 1994). Manuscript No. 1, Box 2, Series 1, Academic Programs and Policies, File #77, Watershed Project, 1994–1995. Armando Arias Archive. Tanimura & Antle Family Memorial Library Archives and Special Collections, California State University Monterey Bay, Seaside, CA.

"A Vision for Learning: Transforming the Paradigm for Higher Education in the 21st Century," (Seaside, CA: 1997): ii–309. [CSUMB Self-study]

"Accord of Mutual Collaboration: A Partnership Between Hartnell College's Social Sciences Department and CSUMB's Center for Social and Behavioral Sciences" (December 12, 1996). Manuscript No. 1, Box 1, Series 1, File 13, Articulation, 1996–1999. Armando Arias Archive. Tanimura & Antle Family Memorial Library Archives and Special Collections, California State University Monterey Bay, Seaside, CA.

Adult Education Act Silver Anniversary, 1966–1991 (Washington, DC: Clearinghouse Division of Adult Education and Literacy, 1991).

Ahmed, Sara. *On Being Included: Racism and Diversity in Institutional Life* (Durham, NC: Duke University Press, 2012).

Alexander, Richard with Robert Knapp, and Bob Filmer, "Program history: Toward Humane Technospheres," 1974–75. Malcolm Stilson Archives and Special Collections, The Evergreen State College, Olympia, WA.

The Articulated Voice: http://ciac.csusb.edu/theArticulatedVoice.html. The official newsletter of the California Intersegmental Articulation Council (CIAC) A professional organization of articulation personnel.

Atwill, Janet M. *Rhetoric Reclaimed: Aristotle and the Liberal Arts Tradition* (Ithaca, NY: Cornell University Press, 1998).

Atwill, Janet M. and Janice M. Lauer (Eds.). *Perspectives on Rhetorical Invention* (Knoxville: The University of Tennessee Press, 2002).

Ballif, Michelle. "Writing the Third-Sophistic Cyborg: Periphrasis on an [In]Tense Rhetoric," *Rhetoric Society Quarterly* 28, no. 4 (1998): 51–72.

Barnard, Frederick A.P. *Annual Report of the President* (New York: Columbia University, 1882).

Barnes, John B. and Gerald R. Reed (Eds.). *The Emerging State College: Boise State College Seminar Dialogue*. Boise, ID: Monograph no. 1 (1969).

Bascom, John. "A Christian State," Address given at University of Wisconsin, June 19, 1887 (Milwaukee, WI: Cramer, Aikens & Cramer, 1887).

———. "Changes in College Life, *The Atlantic* 91 (1903): 749–758.

———. "Education and the State," Address given at the University of Wisconsin (June 17th, 1877).

———. *Things Learned by Living* (New York and London: G.P. Putnam's Sons, The Knickerbocker Press, 1913).

Biesecker, Barbara A. *Addressing Postmodernity: Kenneth Burke, Rhetoric, and a Theory of Social Change* (Tuscaloosa: University of Alabama Press, 2000).

———. "Rethinking the Rhetorical Situation from within the Thematic of 'Différance'," *Philosophy & Rhetoric* 22, no. 2 (1989): 110–30.

Bitzer, Lloyd F. "The Rhetorical Situation," *Philosophy & Rhetoric* 1, no. 1(1968): 1–14.

Bledstein, Burton J. *The Culture of Professionalism: The Middle Class and the Development of Higher Education in America* (New York: W.W. Norton & Company, 1978).

Bogart, Quentin J., and Sue I. Murphey, "Articulation in a Changing Higher Education Environment," *Community College Review* 13, no. 2 (1985): 17–22.

Brown, John S., Allan Collins, and Paul Duguid, "Situated Cognition and the Culture of Learning," *Educational Researcher*, 18 (1989): 32–42.

Brumbaugh, Aaron J. "Establishing New Senior Colleges," *Southern Regional Education Board Monograph*, no. 12 (1966).

Burgoon, Michael, Judee K. Heston, and James C. McCroskey. "The Small Group as a Unique Communication Situation," *Messages: A Reader in Human Communication*, Ed. J.M. Civikly (New York: Random House, 1977), 158–166.

Burke, Kenneth. *A Rhetoric of Motives* (Berkeley: University of California Press, 1950).

Bush, Vannevar. *Science: The Endless Frontier* (Washington, DC: United States Government Printing Office, 1945).

Cadwallader, Mervyn L. "Experiment at San Jose," A Paper Presented to the Conference on Alternative Higher Education," (The Evergreen State College, Olympia, WA, 1981): 1–43.

California Intersegmental Articulation Council, *California Articulation Policies and Procedures Handbook* (2006).

California State Colleges. *Biennium Report of State Colleges to State Board of Education* (September 15, 1946).

California State University, Monterey Bay. (1994, September 27). CSUMB vision statement. Monterey Bay, Seaside, CA.

Canby, Henry Seidel. *Alma Mater: The Gothic Age of the American College* (New York: Farrar & Rinehart, 1936).

Carey, Kevin. *The End of College: Creating the Future of Learning and the University of Everywhere* (New York: Riverhead Books, 2016).

Carnegie Commission on Higher Education. "A Chance to Learn: An Action Agenda for Equal Opportunity in Higher Education" (Hightstown, NJ: McGraw-Hill Book Company, 1970).

Carnegie Commission on Higher Education, "Less Time, More Options," (Hightstown, NJ: McGraw-Hill Book Company, 1971).

Carnegie Commission on Higher Education. "The Open-Door Colleges: Policies for Community Colleges," (Hightstown, NJ: McGraw-Hill Book Company, 1970).

Carnegie Council on Policy Studies in Higher Education. *Three Thousand Futures: The Next Twenty Years for Higher Education* (San Francisco: Jossey-Bass, 1980).

Carnegie Foundation for the Advancement of Teaching. "State Higher Education in California," (Sacramento: California State Printing Office, 1932).

Carpenter, Hazen C. "Emerson, Eliot, and the Elective System" *The New England Quarterly* 24, no. 1 (1951): 13–34.

"Center for Arts, Human Communication, and Creative Technologies Academic Philosophy and Programs" (August 2, 1995): 9; Manuscript No. 1, Box 1, Series 1, Academic Programs and Policies, File #20, Centers & Institutions, 1995–1996. Armando Arias Archive. Tanimura & Antle Family Memorial Library Archivees and Special Collections, California State University Monterey Bay, Seaside, CA.

Chance, William. "A Vision in Progress: The Decision to Establish a Public University at Monterey Bay, An Occasional Paper" (San Jose, CA: California Higher Education Policy Center, 1997).

Chávez, Karma R. *Queer Migration Politics: Activist Rhetoric and Coalitional Possibilities* (Carbondale: University of Illinois Press, 2013).

Clabaugh, Dean E. "The Evergreen State College Developmental Aspects Prior to Appointment of the President," (Olympia, WA: November 25, 1969): 1–11.

———. "Planning for The Evergreen State College: History and Progress," (Olympia, WA: June 15, 1970): 1–32.

Cohen, Arthur M. "The Community Colleges and the Path to the Baccalaureate," (Berkeley, CA: Center for Studies in Higher Education, 2003).

Cohen, Herman. *The History of Speech Communication: The Emergence of a Discipline, 1914–1945* (Annandale, VI: Speech Communication Association, 1995).

Coleman, James S. "The Concept of Equality of Educational Opportunity," *Harvard Educational Review* 38, no. 1 (1968): 7–22.

Comaroff, Jean and John. "Ethnography on an Awkward Scale: Postcolonial Anthropology and the Violence of Abstraction," *Ethnography* 4, no. 2 (2003): 147–79.

Conquergood, Dwight. "Rethinking Ethnography: Towards a Critical Cultural Politics," *Communication Monographs* 58 (1991): 179–194.

Cooper, Troy B. "The Impromptu Rhetorical Situation," *Communication Teacher* 33, no. 4 (2019): 262–65.

Cornell University. *Annual Report to the Board of Trustees* (Ithaca, NY: 1881).

Craig, Robert. "Communication," *Encyclopedia of Rhetoric*, Ed. Thomas O. Sloane (Oxford University Press, 2001), 125–37.

Crowley, Sharon. "Of Gorgias and Grammatology," *College Composition and Communication* 30 (1979): 279–83.

"CSU Office of the Chancellor News Release." (March 17, 1993): Manuscript No. 1, Box 7, Series 8, Misc Subjects, File #9, Fort Ord Campus Initiative, 1993–1994. Armando Arias Archive. Tanimura & Antle Family Memorial Library Archives and Special Collections, California State University Monterey Bay, Seaside, CA.

Curti, Merle and Vernon Carstenson. *The University of Wisconsin: A History, 1848–1925, Volume 1* (Madison: University of Wisconsin Press, 1949).

Dannels, Deanna P. "Communication across the Curriculum Problematics and Possibilities: Standing at the Forefront of Educational Reform," *The Sage Handbook of Communication and Instruction*. Eds. Deanna L. Fassett and John T. Warren (Thousand Oaks, CA: Sage 2010), 55–79.

———. "Leaning In and Letting Go," *Communication Education* 54, no. 1 (2005): 1–5.

———. "Time to Speak Up: A Theoretical Framework of Situated Pedagogy and Practice for Communication across the Curriculum," *Communication Education* 50, no. 2 (2001): 144–58.

Darling, Ann L., and Deanna P. Dannels. "Practicing Engineers Talk about the Importance of Talk: A Report on the Role of Oral Communication in the Workplace," *Communication Education* 52, no. 1 (2003): 1–16.

de Certeau, Michel. *The Practice of Everyday Life*, Trans. Steven Rendall (Berkeley: University of California Press, 1984).

DeMillo, Richard A., and A. J. Young. *Revolution in Higher Education: How a Small Band of Innovators Will Make College Accessible and Affordable* (Boston, MA: MIT Press, 2015).

Derrida, Jacques. *Who's Afraid of Philosophy?; Right to Philosophy I*, Trans. Jan Plug (CA: Stanford University Press, 2002).

Deutsch, Monroe E., Aubrey A. Douglass, and George D. Strayer. "Report of a Survey of the Needs of California in Higher Education," 1948: http://oac.cdlib.org/ark:/13030/hb2p3004kd/?brand=oac4

Dewey, John. *Experience and Education* (Detroit, MI: Free Press, 1938).

Díaz, Eva. *The Experimenters: Chance and Design at Black Mountain College* (Chicago: University of Chicago Press, 2015).

Dolmage, Jay. "'Breathe Upon Us an Even Flame': Hephaestus, History, and the Body of Rhetoric," *Rhetoric Review* 25, no. 2 (2006): 119–40.

Douglass, John A. "The Carnegie Commission and Council on Higher Education: A Retrospective" (Berkeley, CA: Center for Studies in Higher Education, 2005).

Elliot, Charles W. "The Elective System: How to Transform a College with One Uniform Curriculum into a University" (1885): http://www.higher-ed.org/resources/Charles_Eliot.htm

———. "Inaugural Address as President of Harvard, 1869," *Educational Reform* (New York: The Century Co., 1898): 1–38.

———. "The New Education: Its Organization," *The Atlantic* (February 1869):https://www.theatlantic.com/magazine/archive/1869/02/the-new-education/309049/

The Elizabeth Cleaners Street School. *Starting Your Own High School* (New York: Random House, 1972).

"The Evergreen State College at a Glance" (Olympia, WA: 1970). Malcolm Stilson Archives and Special Collections, The Evergreen State College, Olympia, WA.

"The Evergreen State College 1971–72 Bulletin" (Olympia, WA). Malcolm Stilson Archives and Special Collections, The Evergreen State College, Olympia, WA.

"The Evergreen State College: Facts, Figures, and Forecasts for the Future" (September 1970). Malcolm Stilson Archives and Special Collections, The Evergreen State College, Olympia, WA.

The Evergreen State College Planning Conference, February 8–9, 1970, Tape I. 1, Side A. Malcolm Stilson Archives and Special Collections, The Evergreen State College, Olympia, WA.

Farland, Ronnald W. "Proposals for Strengthening the Associate Degree in the California Community Colleges." (1985).

Farland, Ronnald W., and Connie Anderson. "Transfer and Articulation with Four-Year Colleges and Universities: A Report." Sacramento: Office of the Chancellor, California Community Colleges, 1989.

Fashing, Joseph, and Steven E. Deutsch. *Academics in Retreat: The Politics of Educational Innovation* (Albuquerque: University of New Mexico Press, 1971).

Fish, Stanley. *Doing What Comes Naturally: Change, Rhetoric, and the Practice of Theory in Literary and Legal Studies* (Durham: Duke University Press, 1989).

———. *Save the World on Your Own Time* (London: Oxford University Press, 2012).

Five Experimental Colleges: Bensalem, Antioch-Putney, Franconia, Old Westbury, Fairhaven, ed. Gary B. MacDonald (New York: Harper & Row, 1973).

Frost, Susan H. "Historical and Philosophical Foundations for Academic Advising," *Academic Advising: A Comprehensive Handbook*. Eds. Virginia N. Gordon, Wesley R. Habley, and Associates (San Francisco, CA: Jossey-Bass, 2000), 3–17.

"Future Academic plans for minority people at TESC," Letter dated April 19, 1972. Malcolm Stilson Archives and Special Collections, The Evergreen State College, Olympia, WA.

Gabriela, Joseph. "A Vision of the Future: Painting the New Face of CSUMB," *Otter Realm* (September 18, 2014).

Garside, Colleen. "Seeing the Forest through the Trees: A Challenge Facing Communication Across the Curriculum Programs," *Communication Education* 51, no. 1 (2001): 51–64.

Geiger, Roger L. "The Era of Multipurpose Colleges in American Higher Education, 1850–1890." *The American College in the Nineteenth Century*. Ed. Roger L. Geiger (Nashville, TN: Vanderbilt University Press, 2000), 127–52.

———."The Rise and Fall of Useful Knowledge: Higher Education for Science, Agriculture, and the Mechanic Arts, 1850–1875." *The American College in the Nineteenth Century*. Ed. Roger L. Geiger (Nashville, TN: Vanderbilt University Press, 2000), 153–68.

Gehrke, Pat J. "Paladins, Mercenaries, and Practicable Pedagogy." *Communication and Critical/Cultural Studies* 6, no. 4 (2009): 416–20.

Gerth, Donald R. *The People's University: A History of the California State University* (Berkeley, CA: Berkeley Public Policy Press, 2010).

Giamatti, A. Bartlett. *A Free and Ordered Space: The Real World of the University* (New York: W.W. Norton & Company, 1988).

Gilman, Daniel C. "The Benefits Which Society Derives from Universities," *Nature 33*, no. 847 (1886): 281–83. Address given on February 23, 1885 at Johns Hopkins University (Baltimore, MD: Publication Agency of the Johns Hopkins University, 1886), 3–40.

———. "The Building of the University." An Inaugural Address Delivered at Oakland November 7th, 1872. (San Francisco, CA: John H. Carmany & Co. Book and Job Printers).

———. "On the Growth of American Colleges and the Present Tendency to the Study of Science," An Address Delivered at the Dedication of the Sibley College, June 21, 1871 (Ithaca, NY: Cornell University, 1872).

———. "Higher Education in the United States," *University Problems in the United States* (New York: The Century Co., 1898), 289–310.

Giroux, Henry A. "Cultural Studies, Public Pedagogy, and the Responsibility of Intellectuals, *"Communication and Critical/Cultural Studies* 1, no. 1 (2004): 59–79.

Glenny, Lyman A. *Autonomy of the Public Colleges: The Challenge of Coordination* (New York: McGraw-Hill, 1959).

Goldsmith, Sharon S. "Beyond Restructuring: Building a University for the 21st Century," Paper presented for the Annual Meeting of the Association for the Study of Higher Education, (Orland, FL: November 3, 1995), 18–19.

Goodchild, Lester F. "G. Stanley Hall and the Study of Higher Education," *The Review of Higher Education* 20, no. 1 (1996): 69–99.

Graubard, Allen. *Free the Children: Radical Reform and the Free School Movement* (New York: Vintage Books, 1972).

Gries, George A. "Agricultural Programs in California Public Higher Education," (Sacramento: California State Coordinating Council for Higher Education, 1971).

Hall, G. Stanley. "Clark University," *Science* ns-15.362 (January 10, 1890): 18–22.

———. "Contemporary University Problems," *The Pedagogical Seminary* 21, no. 2 (1914): 242–255.

———. "First Annual Report of the President to the Board of Trustees," (Worchester, MA: October 4, 1890).

———. "Second Annual Report of the President to the Board of Trustees," (Worchester, MA: September 29, 1891): 3–15.

———. Editorial, *Pedagogical Seminary* 1, no. 1 (1891a): 121–125.

———. Editorial, *Pedagogical Seminary* 1, no. 3 (1891c): 310–326.

———. "Third Annual Report of the President to the Board of Trustees," (April 1893). Box 77, Presidential Reports. Archives and Special Collections, Clark University, Worchester, MA.

———. "Plans and Work at Clark University," *Science* ns-16.402 (October 17, 1890): 211–214. [Preamble to the First Annual Report of the President].

Harper, William Rainey. *The Prospects of the Small College* (Chicago: University of Chicago Press, 1900).

Hawhee, Debra. *Bodily Arts: Rhetoric and Athletics in Ancient Greece* (Austin: University of Texas Press, 2004).

———. "Kairotic Encounters," *Perspectives on Rhetorical Invention.* Eds. Janet M. Atwill and Janice M. Lauer (Knoxville: The University of Tennessee Press, 2002), 16–35.

Hawkins, Hugh. "University Identity: the Teaching and Research Functions." Eds. Alexandra Oleson, and John Voss, *The Organization of Knowledge in Modern America, 1860–1920* (Baltimore, MD: The Johns Hopkins University Press, 1979), 285–312.

———. *Pioneer: A History of the Johns Hopkins University, 1874–1889* (Ithaca, NY: Cornell University Press, 1960).

Heller, Louis G. *The Death of the American University: With Special Reference to the Collapse of City College of New York* (New York: Arlington House, 1973).

Heller, Nathan, "Laptop U: Has the Future of College Moved Online?" *The New Yorker* 20 (May 2013): 81–91.

Heyns, Garrett. "President of Southwestern Washington State College Committee, at joint public hearing of Senate and House Committees on Higher Education, in House Chamber," (Olympia, WA: 7:30 p.m., February 15, 1967).

Hoeveler, David Jr. "The University and the Social Gospel: The Intellectual Origins of the 'Wisconsin Idea,'" *The Wisconsin Magazine of History* 59, no. 4 (1976): 282–298.

Hossler, Don, Doug Shapiro, Afet Dundar, Mary Ziskin, Jin Chen, Desiree Zerquera, and Vasti Torres. "Transfer & Mobility: A National View of the Pre-Degree Student Movement in Postsecondary Institutions," (National Student Clearinghouse Research Center, 2012).

Hutchins, Robert M. *Higher Learning in America* (New Haven, CT: Yale University Press, 1936).

Illich, Ivan. *Deschooling Society* (New York: Harper & Row, 1970).

Jencks, Chrisopher and David Riesman, *The Academic Revolution* (Garden City, NJ: Doubleday, 1968).

Johnson, Hans. "Higher Education in California: New Goals for the Master Plan," (San Francisco: Public Policy Institute of California, 2010).

Johnson, Stephanie Anne. "Toward a Celebratory and Liberating System of Teaching Public Art," *The Practice of Public Art.* Eds. Cameron Cartiere and Shelly Willis (New York: Routledge, 2008).

Jones, Richard M., *Experiment at Evergreen* (Cambridge, MA: Schenkman Books, 1981).

Kahan, Linda, Chester Royse, and Peter Taylor. "Life on Earth Program History, 1973." Malcolm Stilson Archives and Special Collections, The Evergreen State College, Olympia, WA.

Kamenetz, Anya. *DIY U: Edupunks, Edupreneurs, and the Coming Transformation of Higher Education* (Hartford, VT: Chelsea Green Publishing, 2010).

Kant, Immanuel. *The Conflict of the Faculties*, trans, Mary J. Gregor (University of Nebraska Press, 1992).

Kimball, Bruce A. *Orators and Philosophers: A History of the Idea of Liberal Education* (New York: College Board, 1995).

Kintzer, Frederick C. *Middleman in Higher Education: Improving Articulation among High Schools, Community Colleges, and Senior Institutions* (San Francisco: Jossey-Bass Publishers, 1973).

Kisker, Carrie B., Arthur M. Cohen, and Richard L. Wagoner. *Reforming Transfer and Articulation in California: Four Statewide Solutions for Creating a More Successful and Seamless Transfer Path to the Baccalaureate* (Los Angeles, CA: Center for the Study of Community Colleges, 2010).

Kittler, Friedrich. "Universities: Wet, Hard, Soft, and Harder," *Critical Inquiry* 31, no. 1 (2004): 244–255.

Knoell, Dorothy M., and Leland L. Medsker. "From Junior to Senior College: A National Study of the Transfer Student," (Washington, DC: American Council on Education, 1965): v–102.

Koltai, Leslie. *Redefining the Associate Degree* (Washington, DC: American Association of Community and Junior Colleges, 1984).

Kozol, Jonathan. *Free Schools* (New York: Bantam Books, 1972).

Lanham, Richard A. *The Electronic Word: Democracy, Technology, and the Arts* (Chicago: University of Chicago Press, 1995).

———. "The Rhetorical Paideia: The Curriculum as a Work of Art." *College English* 48, no. 2 (1986): 132–41.

Lave, Jean. *Apprenticeship in Critical Ethnographic Practice* (Chicago: University of Chicago Press, 2011).

———. "Situated Learning in Communities of Practice." *Perspectives on Socially Shared Cognition.* Eds. Lauren B. Resnick, John M. Levine, and Stephanie D. Teasley (American Psychological Association, 1991): 63–83.

Lave, Jean, and E. Wenger. *Situated Learning: Legitimate Peripheral Participation* (London: Cambridge University Press, 1991).

LeFevre, Karen Burke. *Invention as a Social Act* (Carbondale: Southern Illinois University Press, 1987).

Levin, Richard C. *The Worth of the University* (New Haven, CT: Yale University Press, 2013).

Lewis, David L. *W. E. B. Du Bois: Biography of a Race 1868–1919* (New York: Henry Holt, 1993).

MacDonald, Michael. "Encomium of Hegel," *Philosophy & Rhetoric* 39, no. 1 (2006): 22–44.

Marr, David, and S.R. "Rudy" Martin, "M 'n M Manifesto: My Snowman's Burning Down" (March 9, 1972).

McKeon, Richard. *Rhetoric: Essays in Invention and Discovery* (Woodbridge, CT: Ox Bow Press, 1987).

McKinnon, Sara L., Robert Asen, Karma R. Chávez, and Robert Glenn Howard. *text + FIELD: Innovations in Rhetorical Method* (University Park: Pennsylvania University Press, 2016).

McCann, Charles J., 3. Malcolm Stilson Archives and Special Collections, The Evergreen State College, Olympia, WA, 1971, http://archives.evergreen.edu/1971/1971-01/mccann_institutionalgoals.pdf.

———. Malcolm Stilson Archives and Special Collections, The Evergreen State College, Olympia, WA, 1967, http://www.evergreen.edu/facultydevelopment/docs/ABriefHistory1967-73Kormondy.pdf.

———. "Institutional Goals and Statement of Purpose," 2. No date. Malcolm Stilson Archives and Special Collections, The Evergreen State College, Olympia, WA, http://archives.evergreen.edu/1971/1971-01/mccann_institutionalgoals.pdf.

McCarthy, Charles. *The Wisconsin Idea* (New York: The MacMillan Co, 1912).

McConnell, T.R., and T.C. Holy. "A Restudy of the Needs of California Higher Education," (Sacramento: California State Department of Education, 1955) http://www.oac.cdlib.org/view?docId=hb2n39n7ns&brand=oac4&chunk.id=meta.

Medardo, Delgago, Rudolph Martin, and Darrell Phare. "Contemporary American Minorities Program History—Self Evaluation, Faculty Edition," 1972. Malcolm Stilson Archives and Special Collections, The Evergreen State College, Olympia, WA.

Meiklejohn, Alexander. *The Experimental College* (Madison: University of Wisconsin Press, 1932).

Miller, Carolyn R. "Aristotle's 'Special Topics' in Rhetorical Practice and Pedagogy," *Rhetoric Society Quarterly* 17 (Winter 1987): 61–70.

———. "The Aristotelian Topos: Hunting for Novelty," in *Rereading Aristotle's Rhetoric*, eds. Alan G. Gross and Arthur E. Walzer (Carbondale: Southern Illinois University Press, 2000):

Miller, Ron. *Free Schools, Free People: Education and Democracy after the 1960s* (Albany: State University of New York Press, 2002).

Minicucci, Catherine. "An Evaluation of the Transfer Center Pilot Program, Volume 1," (Berkeley, CA: Berman, Weiler Associates, 1989).

Morreale, Sherwyn P. "Communication across the Curriculum and in Undergraduate Education Debated and Clarified," *Spectra 33*, no. 4 (1997): 5–14.

Morreale, Sherwyn P., Michael M. Osborn, and Judy C. Pearson. "Why Communication Is Important: A Rationale for the Centrality of the Study of Communication," *JACA-ANNANDALE-* 1 (2000): 1–25.

Morreale, Sherwyn P., Pamela Shockley-Zalabak, and Penny Whitney. "The Center for Excellence in Oral Communication: Integrating Communication across the Curriculum," *Communication Education 42*, no. 1 (1993): 10–21.

Mosholder, Richard S., and Christopher J. Zirkle. "Historical Trends of Articulation in America: A Review of the Literature," *Community College Journal of Research and Practice* 31, no. 9 (2007): 731–45.

Muckelbauer, John. *The Future of Invention: Rhetoric, Postmodernism, and the Problem of Change* (Albany: State University of New York Press, 2008).

Murphy, Troy A. "Deliberative Civic Education and Civil Society: A Consideration of Ideals and Actualities in Democracy and Communication Education," *Communication Education* 53, no. 1 (2004).

Neill, A.S. *Summerhill: A Radical Approach to Child Rearing* (New York: Hart Publishing, 1960).

Newfield, Christopher. *Unmaking the Public University: The Forty-Year Assault on the Middle Class* (Cambridge, MA: Harvard University Press, 2008).

Nichols, Dick. "A History of Evergreen from Newspaper Headlines," Pack Forest Faculty Retreat, 1972. Video edited by D.F. Smith. The Evergreen Visual History Collection, Malcolm Stilson Archives and Special Collections, The Evergreen State College, Olympia, WA: http://blogs.evergreen.edu/visualhistory/?p=568

Nietzsche, Friedrich. *On the Future of Our Educational Institutions* (South Bend, IN: St. Augustine's Press, 2004).

Nussbaum, Martha C. *Cultivating Humanity: A Classical Defense of Reform in Liberal Education* (Cambridge, MA: Harvard University Press, 1997).

Odell, Morgan. "Distribution of Authority with the California State College System," (Ph.D. dissertation, University of Southern California, 1967).

O'Halloran, Sinon Kevin. *Alexis Frederick Lange, Pioneer in California Education 1890–1924: His Influence and Impact on an Evolving State School System* (Berkeley: University of California Press, 1987).

Ohl, Jessy J. "Reinvigorating Civic Education in Communication Through *Imitatio*," *Communication Teacher* (2020): 1–5.

Otten, Alan L. "Politics and People," *Wall Street Journal* (December 20, 1973).

Peters, John Durham. *Speaking into the Air: A History of the Idea of Communication* (Chicago: University of Chicago Press, 1999).

Peters, Scott J., Theodore R. Alter, and Neil Schartzbach. *Democracy and Higher Education: Traditions and Stories of Civic Engagement* (East Lansing: Michigan State University Press, 2010).

Phelps, Louise Wetherbee. "Institutional Invention: (How) Is It Possible?," *Perspectives on Rhetorical Invention*. Eds. Janet M. Atwill and Janice M. Lauer (Knoxville: The University of Tennessee Press, 2002): 64–95.

Philipsen, Gerry. "Paying Lip Service to 'Speech' in Disciplinary Naming, 1914–1954," *A Century of Communication Studies: The Unfinished Conversation*. Eds. William M. Keith and Pat J. Gehrke (New York: Routledge, 2014): 58–75.

Radway, Janice. "Research Universities, Periodical Publication, and the Circulation of Professional Expertise: On the Significance of Middlebrow Authority," *Critical Inquiry* 31, no. 1 (2004): 203–28.

Readings, Bill. *The University in Ruins* (Cambridge, MA: Harvard University Press, 1996).

Remnick, Noah. "Yale Grapples with Ties to Slavery in a Debate Over a College's Name," *The New York Times* (September 11, 2015): http://www.nytimes.com/2015/09/12/nyregion/yale-in-debate-over-calhoun-college-grapples-with-ties-to-slavery.html?_r=0.

Reuben, Julie A. *The Making of the Modern University: Intellectual Transformation and the Marginalization of Morality* (Chicago: University of Chicago Press, 1996).

Rousseau, Jean-Jacques, *Emile, or On Education*, trans., Allan Bloom (New York: Basic Books, 1979).

Ryan, W. Carson. *Studies in Early Graduate Education: The John Hopkins, Clark University, The University of Chicago* (Boston, MA: The Merrymount Press, 1939).

Sandison, Gordon. Paraphrased in the August 30, 1967 Minutes of the Board of Trustees New Four Year College, Office of the Governor, Olympia, Washington. Malcolm Stilson Archives and Special Collections, The Evergreen State College, Olympia, WA.

Scott, James C. *Seeing Like a State: How Certain Schemes to Improve the Human Condition Have Failed* (New Haven, CT: Yale University Press, 1998).

Sefton-Green, Julian. "Cultural Studies and Education: Reflecting on Differences, Impacts, Effects and Change," *Cultural Studies* 25, no. 1 (2011): 55–70.

Shenk, Gerald E. "Requiem for a Vision in Higher Education," Unpublished manuscript (Seaside, CA: September 2014).

Shils, Edward. *The Order of Learning: Essays on the Contemporary University* (New Brunswick, NJ: Transaction Publishers, 1997).

Shoben, Joseph. "Some thoughts, mostly random, about both buildings and academic program," Memorandum dated October 13, 1969 addressed to President McCann. Malcolm Stilson Archives and Special Collections, The Evergreen State College, Olympia, WA.

———. "Another pass at academic organization and the curriculum at TESC," Memorandum dated November 10, 1969 addressed to President Charles McCann and Vice Presidents David Barry and Dean Clabaugh. Malcolm Stilson Archives and Special Collections, The Evergreen State College, Olympia, WA.

Silva, Elena, Taylor White, and Thomas Toch. "The Carnegie Unit: A Century-Old Standard in a Changing Education Landscape," (Stanford, CA: Carnegie Foundation for the Advancement of Teaching, 2015).

Simonson, Peter. "Reinventing Invention, Again," *Rhetoric Society Quarterly* 44, no. 4 (2014): 299–322.

Smith, John E. "Time, Times, and the 'Right Time': 'Chronos' and 'Kairos,'" *The Monist* 53, no. 1 (January 1969): 1–13.

Sprague, Jo. "Ontology, Politics, and Instructional Communication Research: Why We Can't Just "Agree to Disagree" About Power," *Communication Education, 43*, no. 4 (1994): 273–290.

————. "Retrieving the Research Agenda for Communication Education: Asking the Pedagogical Questions That Are "Embarrassments to Theory," *Communication Education* 42, no. 2 (1993): 106–122.

Stark, Jack. *The Wisconsin Idea: The University's Service to the State*. Reprinted from the 1995–1996 Wisconsin Blue Book (Madison, WI: Legislative Reference Bureau, 1995).

Steffens, Lincoln. "Sending a State to College: What the University of Wisconsin Is Doing for Its People," *The American Magazine* 67 (1909).

Stephens, Dale L. *"Kairos* and the Rhetoric of Belief," *Quarterly Journal of Speech* 78 (1992): 317–332.

Stevens III, William Henry. "The Philosophical and Political Origins of the Evergreen State College" (PhD diss., University of Washington, 1983).

Swidler, Ann. *Organization Without Authority: Dilemmas of Social Control in Free Schools* (Cambridge, MA: Harvard University Press, 1979).

Tebbel, John. *The Expansion of an Industry, 1865–1919: Vol. 2 of a History of Book Publishing in the United States* (New York: R.R. Bowker, 1975).

Teitelbaum, Herta. "Anticipating, Implementing, and Adapting to Changes in Academic Advising," *Academic Advising: A Comprehensive Handbook*. Eds. Virginia N. Gordon, Wesley R. Habley, and Associates (San Francisco, CA: Jossey-Bass, 2000), 393–408.

Thoreau, Henry David. *Walden, or Life in the Woods* (Boston, MA: Ticknor and Fields, 1854).

Travers, Paul D. "G. Stanley Hall: Pioneer in Comparative Education," *The Educational Forum* 33, no. 3 (1969): 301–305.

University of California, Berkeley All-University Faculty Conference, "The Research Function of the University: Proceedings," (Riverside: University of California, 1960).

"University Learning Requirements" (June 1996), Manuscript No. 1, Box 2, Series 1, File 75, Folder ii. Armando Arias Archive. Tanimura & Antle Family Memorial Library Archives and Special Collections, California State University Monterey Bay, Seaside, CA.

Untersteiner, Mario. *The Sophists*, trans. Kathleen Freeman (Oxford: Blackwell, 1954).

Vasconcellos, John and the Joint Committee for Review of the Master Plan for Higher Education. "California Faces . . . California's Future: Education for Citizenship in a Multicultural Democracy" (Sacramento: California State Assembly, 1989): http://www.oac.cdlib.org/view?docId=hb2r29n7hc&brand=oac4&doc.view=entire_text

Vatz, Richard E. "The Myth of the Rhetorical Situation," *Philosophy & Rhetoric* 6, no. 3 (1973): 154–161.

Veblen, Thorstein. *The Higher Learning in America: A Memorandum on the Conduct of Universities By Business Men* (New York: B.W. Huebsch, 1918).

Veysey, Lawrence R. *The Emergence of the American University* (Chicago: University of Chicago Press, 1965).

Wattenberger, James L., and Allen A. Witt. "Origins of the California System: How the Junior College Movement Came to California," *Community College Review* 22, no. 4 (1995): 17–25.

Wellman, Jane V., and Thomas Ehrlich. *How the Student Credit Hour Shapes Higher Education: The Tie That Binds* (San Francisco: Jossey-Bass, 2003).

Westmeyer, Paul. *An Analytic History of American Higher Education* (Springfield, IL: Charles C. Thomas, 1997).

White, Eric Charles. *Kaironomia: On the Will to Invent Ithaca* (New York: Cornell University Press, 1987).

Williams, Raymond. *Communications* (New York: Penguin Books, 1962).

Williams, Roger L. *The Origins of Federal Support for Higher Education: George W. Atherton and the Land-Grant College Movement* (University Park: The Pennsylvania State University Press, 1991).

Winter, Carl G. "History of the Junior College Movement in California," Bureau of Junior College Education Release 20 (Sacramento, CA: 1964): 1–43.

Witte, John F. "Wisconsin Ideas: The Continuing Role of the University in the State and Beyond." *New Directions for Higher Education* 112 (Winter 2000): 7–16.

Yost, Mary. "Training Four Minute Men at Vassar." *Quarterly Journal of Speech Education* 5, no. 3 (1919): 246–253.

Youtz, Byron L. "The Evergreen State College: An Experiment Maturing." (1981). Malcolm Stilson Archives and Special Collections, The Evergreen State College, Olympia, WA:http://archives.evergreen.edu/1982/1982-09/Alternative_Ed_Conference-1981/Youtz_B.pdf.

Index

About the Author

Kathleen F. McConnell is professor of rhetorical studies in the Department of Communication Studies at San José State University, affiliated faculty in SJSU's Educational Leadership Program. Her research explores how academic institutions sustain the prospects for invention, and the ways in which educational policies and practices curtail wider participation in inquiry and knowledge production.

Lightning Source UK Ltd.
Milton Keynes UK
UKHW020350030920
369254UK00003B/51